CONTEMPORARY ECONOMICS

A UNIFYING APPROACH

by David Z. Rich

PRAEGER

PRAEGER SPECIAL STUDIES • PRAEGER SCIENTIFIC

New York • Philadelphia • Eastbourne, UK
Toronto • Hong Kong • Tokyo • Sydney

Library of Congress Cataloging-in-Publication Data

Rich, David Z.
Contemporary economics.

Bibliography: p.
Includes index.
1. Economics. I. Title.
HB171.5.R399 1986 330 85-16762
ISBN 0-03-006247-0 (alk. paper)

Published and Distributed by the
Praeger Publishers Division
(ISBN Prefix 0-275)
of Greenwood Press, Inc.,
Westport, Connecticut

Published in 1986 by Praeger Publishers
CBS Educational and Professional Publishing
a Division of CBS Inc.
521 Fifth Avenue, New York, NY 10175 USA

6789 052 987654321

Printed in the United States of America
on acid-free paper

International Offices
Orders from outside the United States should be sent to the appropriate address listed below. Orders from areas not listed below should be placed through CBS International Publishing, 383 Madison Ave., New York, NY 10175 USA
Australia, New Zealand: Holt Saunders, Pty, Ltd., 9 Waltham St., Artarmon, N.S.W. 2064, Sydney, Australia
Canada: Holt, Rinehart & Winston of Canada, 55 Horner Ave., Toronto, Ontario, Canada M8Z 4X6
Europe, the Middle East, & Africa: Holt Saunders, Ltd., 1 St. Anne's Road, Eastbourne, East Sussex, England BN21 3UN
Japan: Holt Saunders, Ltd., Ichibancho Central Building, 22-1 Ichibancho, 3rd Floor, Chiyodaku, Tokyo, Japan
Hong Kong, Southeast Asia: Holt-Saunders Asia, Ltd., 10 Fl, Intercontinental Plaza, 94 Granville Road, Tsim Sha Tsui East, Kowloon, Hong Kong

Manuscript submissions should be sent to the Editorial Director, Praeger Publishers, 521 Fifth Avenue, New York, NY 10175 USA

This work is dedicated to my mother, the memory of my father, to my sisters, family, and friends, and to Diana Lerner, my beautiful Diana.

CONTENTS

PART I
THE PROBLEM SITUATION

For surely if knowledge is to be the foundation for organizing experience, then experience in turn must be continuously projected on knowledge to make us see the meaning of what we know as well as the meaning of what we do.

Peter F. Drucker,
The Age of Discontinuity

INTRODUCTION: ON THE NATURE OF THIS WORK

Traditionally, economics has been the study of the origins and causes of wealth as manifested in the divisions of national product and the relationships between the factors of production and distribution. This tone of economic inquiry was set by Adam Smith and carried over by Keynes in his *General Theory*. This tradition was somewhat altered, however, in the period following World War II, when the economies of scale merged with postwar technology to yield a radically new form of economics, that of managerial capitalism, so that the new aspect of market formulations had to be considered. Thus, industrial control and the employees who worked the plant became equally important with the division of national output among the producing sources. With the expansion and diversification of the giant industries, consumers were more frequently their own employees. Moreover, since labor is a factor of production, it became not uncommon for previously rigid industrial establishments to absorb a talented rank-and-file member into the managerial staff, sometimes employing the individual in dealing with manager-worker relations.

As postwar managerial capitalism developed, new concepts of supply and demand were formulated in which production was relegated to projected demand schedules, allowing for marginal deviations in both consumption and production. Hence, the neoclassical explanation of underconsumption and of overproduction for interpreting business fluctuations lost its import in managerial capitalism.

While managerial economics has made a profound impact on production and consumption, it has an uneasy existence with neo-Keynesian economics. This form of economic reasoning is based on maintaining the economy on an equilibrium growth pattern. It is as if the historic trauma of the Great Depression has become part of the economic psyche so that all forces that disturb equilibrium are viewed at best as suspect and at worst as dangerous.

Dynamic equilibrium has become the watchword of the overseers of the economy, so much so that it has permeated the reasoning of the practitioners of managerial capitalism. This is a paradoxical situation for both the logic of economics and the realities of economic life. Growth, in reference to the corporation and the macro economy, requires shifting production patterns, the phasing out of existing markets, and the development of new markets. This is explained in the chapters that follow; at this point, however, it needs to be mentioned that growth and equilibrium are incompatible positions. An element of uncertainty, manifested as risk is inherent in every economic undertaking; this element, magnified to macro proportions, most certainly makes the notion in economic growth highly questionable.

This work analyzes equilibrium economics in both macroequilibrium reasoning and the managerial micro argument and points out how these two now-conventional approaches to economics have failed, as we are now witnessing. It presents an approach to economics that employs the viable elements of both micro and macro thinking, while discarding those elements unnecessary to economic growth. In addition, based on this new approach, it examines international trade, the emerging and developing economies and the status of their trading positions, and the consideration of neocolonialism and the independence of these developing economies.

1

ON SAY'S LAW OF MARKETS

INTRODUCTION

No economic law has held such celebrated status as the Law of Markets posited by the French economist and follower of Adam Smith, J. B. Say. This law is a refinement of the argument of his British predecessors. John Locke, for example, argued that a higher (that is, meta) economic force regulated the overall balance between production and consumption. David Hume turned to international trade as the vestiges of mercantilism were giving way to more rational approaches to commerce and stated that in a specie-goods flow, imports tend to equal exports with all differences in balance, should they occur, made up in currency payment. Balance, equilibrium—these were the key concepts when Adam Smith wrote the *Wealth of Nations*; the nature of economics during his time as existed in transactions fortified his confidence in balance and equilibrium, both in domestic and international commerce.

Smith sought to explain the forces of economics in terms of their objective manifestations of supply and demand, emphasizing the division of labor as a means of achieving maximum productive efficiency, with the amount of labor employed determined by the demand for the product. Hence, in the economy as understood by Adam Smith, the "invisible hand" of supply and demand leads to the most efficient use of resources and provides the markets the greatest amount of goods and services at the lowest—that is, the most competitive—prices. This efficient operation of market forces depends on the lack of government restrictions as well as on the absence of collusion on the part of both the buyers and sellers of the transactions.

This "invisible hand" was not considered a static force, for it brought about shifts in fortunes. The demand for product A, for example, would be of such intensity that many merchants would enter the market supplying A. This would result in a surplus of A, with demand not keeping pace with supply. Product B would be scarce because of the allocation of resources for A, so that its price would be high relative to A. Profits from marketing B would be high while those for A would be low because of the competition, and merchants would then allocate resources into marketing B because of the high profits. A would still be produced but at lower rates so that its price would rise relative to B, which would now be competitive. Fortunes would thus be made and lost, depending on the intensity of demand, the ability to sell at the lowest price for sufficiently long durations, and the ability to expand and diversify into other products that satisfy consumer demand. Given free markets, those businesses that could withstand the rigors of demand would survive and prosper; those that were unable would fail. The "invisible hand" certainly regulated the free markets, but in doing so it often wielded a sharp sword.

The process Adam Smith described was explained by Say. Smith described the workings of the free market but left unraised and therefore unanswered the question that was to present itself to economists ever since: How is demand created? For markets to be regulated by supply and demand, free-market forces had to be generated. The question arose, because of the basis on which supply and demand exist and their relationship to the markets other than merely regulatory. Moreover, as Smith described a process which demystified Locke, he nevertheless did not come to grips with the questions he raised in the *Wealth of Nations*, for while describing the activities of supply and demand he never explained how these forces come about.

This Say did in his Law of Markets. Put simply, Say's Law maintains that supply creates its own demand, so that as supply increases so does demand, and as supply decreases a corresponding decrease in demand occurs. A product is presented in the market and brought to the attention of consumers, who allocate a part of their purchasing power to its consumption. The supply has generated demand; and the greater the demand, the greater will be the increase in production, until no increase in neither supply nor demand is warranted. Should there be a radical shift in one or both sides of the transaction, then as the product is phased out, demand shifts toward other products and the supply-demand relationship is reinstated. Yet, this simple Law of Markets, which was posited for setting the "invisible hand" in motion, sparked this tirade by Malthus:

> Of all the opinions advanced by able and ingenious men which I have met with, the opinion of M. Say which states that *un produit consommé ou détruit est en debouche fermé* (I. i. ch. 15) appears to me to be the most directly opposed to just theory, and the most uniformly contradicted by experience. Yet it directly follows from new doctrine, that commodities are to be considered only in their relation to each other, —not to the consumers. What, I would ask, would become of the demand for commodities, if all consumption except bread and water were suspended for the next half-year? *Quels débouches*! What a prodigious market would this event occasion.[1]

Prodigious indeed, but not in keeping with Say's Law, nor with Smith's "invisible hand." Malthus did not mention in this comment that those who produce the nation's wealth are also, in the aggregate, the consumers of this very wealth. Given unrestricted market conditions, those products would not be marketed if they were not consumed; thus, the only thing prodigious about the market would be the diversified products available to suit the varied tastes and incomes of the consuming public.

It must also be noted that the "just theory" that Malthus considered in opposition to Say's Law is his very own—the specter of which still lingers over the world. The poverty Malthus's theory foretold could not argue away the use of aggregate supply-and-demand functions reaching equilibrium through the equation of supply with demand, for Malthus's argument was based on the ability of the soil to feed a population that expanded during periods of prosperity, reaching numbers greater than the agricultural yields could feed.

The prophecy of doom that Malthus predicted has been kept at bay by wars that have depleted the population and by technology that has increased the agricultural yield per acre of farmed land. Should there be a world catastrophe, these techniques would break down, making the existence of a Malthusian condition highly probable. Such calamities as world war or severe worldwide drought could result in the condition Malthus described as being the consequence of population pressure on scarce food supplies.

However, Say's law—posited in *A Treatise on Political Economy* (1803)—did break down, this during the Great Depression. Its validity was brought into question by Keynes, who wrote that if Say's Law were not the true law relating the aggregate demand-and-supply functions, "then there is a vitally important chapter of economic theory which remains to be rewritten and without which all discussions concerning the volume of aggregate employment are futile."[2] Keynes's argument brought Say's Law into the forefront of argument, where before it had been a cornerstone of economic reasoning. The faith in the Law of Markets perhaps contributed to the existence and duration of the Great Depression.

SAY'S LAW AND KEYNES'S ARGUMENT

Keynes's argument against Say's Law of markets proceeds thus: Let Z be the aggregate supply price of output whose production requires N men, with the relationship between Z and N being $Z = \phi(N)$, which is the aggregate supply function. Similarly, let D be the proceeds entrepreneurs expect to receive from the employment of N men,[3] so that $D = f(N)$, which is the aggregate demand function.

For a given value of N if the expected proceeds are greater than the aggregate supply price, that is, if D is greater than Z, there will be an incentive to increase employment beyond N and if necessary to raise costs by competing for the factors of production up to the value of N for which Z becomes equal to D. At this point of intersection between the aggregate supply-and-demand functions the amount of employment is fixed; Keynes said that at this point the entrepreneur's expectation of profits (but not necessarily the profits themselves) will be maximized.

Keynes challenges the classical argument: Say's Law, stating that supply creates its own demand, involves a special assumption about the aggregate supply-and-demand functions, that being that $f(N)$ and $\phi(N)$ are equal for all values of N and that therefore an increase in $Z = \phi(N)$ corresponding to an increase in N necessitates an increase in $D = f(N)$ by the same amount as Z. This means that instead of having a unique equilibrium value, effective demand is at an infinite range of values, each equally admissible as equilibrium points. Furthermore, should this condition hold, competition would always lead to the expansion of employment to the point where an increase in effective demand will no longer effect an increase in employment, which amounts to the same thing as continuous full employment. Here, Malthus's comment that Say's Law is not in accordance with economic reasoning rings true, for the Law of Markets as analyzed by Keynes most certainly did not hold for the Great Depression.[4]

SAY'S LAW AND EQUILIBRIUM ANALYSIS

In spite of Malthus's criticism, Say's Law of Markets served as the cornerstone for classical and neoclassical economics—what Keynes called orthodox economics—and owes its durability to the fact that until the Great Depression conditions existed which were within the confines of Say's Law. Supply did generate demand, and demand had reinforced the output of supply. The elasticity of supply depended on effective demand as expressed through aggregate purchases, that is, through consumption; the elasticity of demand was determined by the quantity of supply and the available alternatives for consumption. The orthodox economists attributed fluctuations, not to the breakdown of Say's Law, but to the intervention of noneconomic factors and the restrictions on competition due to monopolistic and oligopolistic practices and to government policy.[5]

Say's Law had achieved such wide acceptance also because of the newness of economics as a discipline. Say explained the relationship between supply and demand, taking Smith's "invisible hand" as the market regulator and reducing it to a causal relationship between supply and demand. Employment led to the production of goods and services, with labor receiving remuneration for its output. The money had to be spent consuming the existing supplies of these very goods and services. That portion of wages not spent, that is, wages saved, was invested in financial institutions (hoarding being marginal) to be placed at the disposal of firms for retooling and manufacturing. The time interval between retooling and manufacturing was of little consequence for the orthodox economists, for the aggregate demand-and-supply curves were affected very little during these intervals. The orthodox economists held the point that in the long run all economic fluctuations would level out, with growth curves moving upward and outward. The orthodox economists thus minimized fluctuations, only to be without nonorthodox explanations for the intensity and duration of the Great Depression.

In light of the economic history of the capitalist countries, before the Great Depression there was little worry over the possible collapse of financial institutions. The central banks were to operate contrary to the prevailing market trends, stemming the tide when the markets became overheated and easing conditions when the markets were slowing down, thereby maintaining the viability of the economy and its institutions. The concern was for maintaining equilibrium in a situation of growth, which was to be guaranteed by the central banks and the government monetary institutions. When the Great Depression hit, however, the theories of central banking broke down. The run on the banks paralyzed the entire financial structure of capitalist countries, with brokerage houses trying to trade off near-worthless stocks to maintain a degree of liquidity. Uncertainty did not remain purely domestic but spread to international commerce, with countries once again returning to the antiquated principles of mercantilism. Devaluations were undertaken for short-term advantages, the gains of which were reduced or eliminated as other countries followed suit. Commerce among nations slowed down, further hindering domestic output and the flow of money within the economies.

All economic recessions and depressions are contrary to Say's Law. Orthodox economists struggled with the difficulties of recessions and depressions, but they failed to challenge the respected Law of Markets, mainly because economics was a relatively new science and they saw no serious contradiction between the scientific law Say posited and minor fluctuations in the workings of economic systems. They reasoned that after all, even in the most exact of the natural sciences acceptable deviations from experimental and theoretical predictions exist, and the science of economics does not operate in the laboratory employing the most stringent of controlled conditions. Hence, the orthodox economists sought to explain the breakdown of Say's Law in terms of political interference in the workings of the markets, cartels, and oligopolies; the restrictive practices of labor organizations; and the general world instability. Although the overproductionists and underconsumptionists questioned the validity of Say's Law, they failed to state their theories within the context of classical and neoclassical reasoning. Keynes, however, argues his case based on classical and neoclassical reasoning, showing where the accepted bodies of knowledge were inoperable for the conditions of the Great Depression and pointing out the invalidity of Say's Law.

Nevertheless, Keynes's argument itself is not free of the taint of invalidity. Consider his argument that demand-and-supply schedules are equal in the aggregate and that as a result all points in the demand-and-supply schedules are equal. This, of course, was Say's point also —that demand and supply are equal for all output and that full employment exists. Keynes rightly stated that according to Say's argument, instead of a single equilibrium position, equilibrium would be total. But why should even a single equilibrium position exist? Surely, within the realm of Great Depression economics—the problem area with which Keynes dealt—equilibrium did not even exist for a single market. Either supply or demand was excessive in relation to the other, but never in balance. Equilibrium describes the relations of economic forces when converging at a specific point of stability. Consider the following comments by Tibor Scitovsky:

> For price takers are people who can transact all the business they want to at the market price; and this means that for all the buyers and all the sellers in the market to be price takers at the same time, the quantities that the buyers want to buy must add up exactly to the sum of the quantities that the sellers want to sell. If this condition is to be fulfilled, the market place must be such as to equate supply with demand.[6]

According to Keynes, where $Z = D$ for each product, there is equilibrium; when the aggregate supply-and-demand functions meet, then aggregate equilibrium is achieved. From the vantage of historical reasoning, the following comments can be made: First, to reach aggregate equilibrium, the supply and demand must be for each product. Second, although these schedules are not infinite, they are as many and as diversified as the products. Third, according to Keynes's comments, for Say's equilibrium to be reached for the aggregate supply-and-demand schedules, the amount of labor must be infinite to account for increased products and increased demand. Keynes failed to account for a fixed or slowly increasing labor force, supplemented by increasingly sophisticated technology for increased production of diversified goods, thereby allowing the greater portion of consumer liquidity to be directed toward demand. No necessary correlation exists between increased production, increased diversity, and an increasing labor force equal to the production and diversity requirements, for these can be and very often are offset by technology.

Moreover, in contemporary economies in the postindustrial era aggregate equilibrium cannot exist. It is ruled out by constantly changing markets, some being introduced and others being phased out while others are still expanding. Also, supply-and-demand schedules are not for single products from a macro perspective but for similar, that is, imitative, products that are manifold variations on a single-product theme. Here, the limit on infinite production for a single product is prohibited by consumption of close substitutes and by the allocation of resources for other product lines.

Furthermore, to say that $Z = D$ in aggregate equilibrium means that for every market m, $Z_1^m = D_1^m$ for the manifold products and markets. At each point of juncture for Z and D and in each specific market m, supply and demand are equal and employment is of sufficient level to maintain this equality. Hence, even taking into account technology's impact on the labor market and on production, the labor force must consume only what is produced, the products marketed *in toto*. Here, therefore, is a case of supply generating its own demand as consumption must relate to production for each *m* and for aggregate equilibrium. Say's Law, criticized by Keynes, has indeed been reinstated by Keynes in the guise of equilibrium reasoning.[7]

The argument presented here is that equilibrium, whether static or dynamic, is inconsistent with the realities of contemporary economics. This is discussed in the chapters that follow, after which is presented a theory unifying the viable aspects of microeconomics and managerial economics with macroeconomics in dynamic disequilibrium.

2

SAY'S LAW AND TWO POST-KEYNESIAN THEORIES

PRELIMINARY COMMENTS

"Our comfortable belief in the efficacy of Say's Law," wrote Evsay Domar, "has been badly shaken in the last fifteen years. Both events and discussions have shown that supply does not automatically create its own demand. A part of income generated by the productive process may not be returned to it; this part may be saved or hoarded."[1] Money saved in the accepted savings institutions will be eventually returned to the productive process, thereby generating goods and services; so, on this point Say's Law maintains a degree of validity. Domar's comment that hoarding is a significant factor is questionable, for it is unprofitable to hoard money because it yields no rate of return and in periods of inflation hoarding is decreased as higher prices bring the money into circulation to compensate for the erosion of value. The focus must be placed on the money in circulation, both the money savings have brought into the economy and the hoarded money brought into circulation and into the money flow. This returns the discussion to Say's Law, as money is the means of exchange on which consumption and production are based.

This chapter focuses on two theories that represent the different directions economic theory has taken since *The General Theory* and the economic reconstruction following World War II. These two theories—the macro theory known as the Harrod-Domar model and the micro theory of managerial capitalism posited by Robin Marris—show the manner by which macro and government economists approach business activity and businesspeople approach their production projects and view market dynamics. Both theories are equilibrium oriented, operating according to Say's Law, and both are growth oriented, seeking to expand their areas of economic activity, phase out those that are not profitable, and in the case of managerial economics develop new market possibilities. As these theories are dynamic-equilibrium based, each in its own right is contradictory to the real issues of economic growth and each results in the establishment of inadequate programs.

In a democratic society equilibrium and growth are contradictory objectives; growth cannot be controlled in equilibrium because businesspeople open new markets and take their risks. Governments in these societies cannot dictate to businesspeople which markets should be developed and which should be phased out or which directions managerial activity should undertake to expand existing markets. Monetary and fiscal policies may be employed to channel economic activity, to cool down the cycle when overextended, and to revive activity after saturation has been removed; these are legitimate procedures for maintaining the economy's viability and should not be employed on the basis of doctrinaire reasoning based on equilibrium.

That dynamic equilibrium is emphasized in these theories is due to the inability of contemporary orthodox economists to realize that the tenets of classical and neoclassical economics are no longer valid in the postindustrial—or to use Zbigniew Brzezinski's term, the "technetronic"[2] —era where growth is a result of market exploitation and equilibrium plays no role in the considerations and programs of managers in the big corporations. Of course, it can be argued that the jobs of government and business differ, that the profit motive brings businesses into all types of markets while at the same time the government seeks to limit the macro economy from reaching overextended levels of erratic growth or too low levels of economic slowdown, thus maintaining some degree of economic equilibrium in the macro economy, ensuring growth without severe economic disruptions. This economic equilibrium is what the Harrod-Domar model seeks to achieve. However, while the intention is sound, the reasoning is no longer valid. Due to the structure of postindustrial societies such economic equilibrium cannot be maintained and the policies of such approaches cannot be applied without serious disruptions occurring, the very disruptions these policies seek to prevent.

THE HARROD-DOMAR MODEL

The Harrod-Domar model is Keynesian in nature because it emphasized the government's role in economic activity.[3] Nevertheless, it entails the basic question raised by Adam Smith, that of the origins and causes of the wealth of nations. It was evidenced during the Great Depression that significant productive capacity can lie idle with a potentially productive work force remaining unemployed. While Keynes's theory provided a solution to the Great Depression, in the aftermath of World War II a different set of problems arose.

There was no serious threat of prolonged recession or depression after the war. There was, however, a decline in economic activity as industry shifted its productive capacity from a wartime footing to peacetime production in anticipation of a large potential aggregate demand to compensate for the decline in demand due to the exigencies of the war. The problem that confronted Harrod and Domar was how to maintain equilibrium growth while keeping output expanding and preventing serious cyclic fluctuations.

The Harrod-Domar model of growth took on added significance for two reasons. First, the cold war and the instability of the defeated countries required programs that when instituted would build up these countries, not in accordance with the competitive requirements of the cold war, but as consumer-oriented societies similar to the victorious countries. This required a macro growth model that would eliminate economic distortions and hence a volatile economic situation that could be exploited by the communist bloc. The defeated countries of Germany and Japan possessed skilled labor and technological potential sufficient for such programs, and the Harrod-Domar model provided a basis for the reconstruction. It was not as if these countries had to begin anew psychologically, for the motivation to forget the trauma of the war and to begin reconstruction was certainly strong. A growth model in which equilibrium could be maintained served the purpose of these countries, with investments allowing industry to be rebuilt and the peoples' inner drives providing the wherewithal for doing the work.

The second reason for this model's added significance is that the countries established in the aftermath of World War II required a growth model that would aid in the channeling of investments into heavy industry without bringing about major economic upheavals that would leave them an easy prey for foreign conquest and domination.

Countries such as India, Pakistan, and the newly formed State of Israel each had its own set of problems, compounded by the search for capital for building industry. The politics of the cold war certainly played a role in these countries' considerations and calculations for the accumulation of capital, and they used these funds as best possible given the internal and external pressures upon them. In consequence, each country required a growth model that would allow for demand to increase with increased supply but that would ensure growth without major disruptions. Such a model as that of Harrod-Domar thus suited the occasion.

In light of the economic depression that existed prior to the war and because of the many economic problems in both the vanquished and victorious countries in the aftermath of the war, the Harrod-Domar model sought to establish the economic determinants of growth necessary to ensure that aggregate demand and aggregate supply would develop in a manner that would continue growth on a pattern devoid as possible of fluctuations. The model emphasizes the role of capital investment in increasing productive capacity and the significance of investments in generating income necessary for providing employment and hence maintaining aggregate supply and demand. The roles of productive capacity and income are such that they must be in balance, in equilibrium, if the economy is to have stable and constant growth. If productive capacity grows more rapidly than income, the result will be unemployment, since inventories are moved at a slower rate than they are produced by the labor force, and labor is reduced to compensate for the lack of sales. There will be unused resources due to increased production, with the consequence being reduced investments. If, on the other hand, income increases faster than output, inflation will result from excess purchasing power unaccompanied by increased output; the consequence of this is also reduced investments.

Hence, increased investments increase both aggregate demand and aggregate supply. Stated notationally, increased investment ΔI leads to increased income ΔY; this increase is in accordance with the standard multiplier equation $Y = I/\Delta l - c$, where c is the marginal propensity to consume. This equation can also take the form $Y = \Delta I/s$, where s is the marginal propensity to save. The economy's additional capacity for output depends on the capital-output ratio, that is, the accelerator. If k dollars of investment are required for creating the capacity of one dollar additional output, it will therefore require $k\Delta Y$ dollars of investment to produce an output increment equal to ΔY, so that $I = k\Delta Y$ and therefore $\Delta Y = l/k$.

The equations in this model representing the marginal propensities to consume and save are the demand equations; those equations pertaining to investment and the accelerator represent the aggregate supply potential. This is aggregate supply *potential* because investment is undertaken with regard both to the present state of the economy and to its prospects in the future—prospects that can only be expected. Moreover, sustained economic growth requires that these equations be equal, so that $\Delta I/s = l/k$; that is, that if there is to be equality between supply and demand, there must be growth at a rate equal to s/k. Since savings (and since Keynes's investment) are assumed to be a constant percentage of Y due to marginal propensities to consume and save, the equation can be written thusly: $\Delta Y/Y = s/k$.

This model purports no automatic self-regulating method for growth. This year's savings and investments (minus hoarding) result in increased incomes next year. Large savings produce large incomes that must be offset again by large savings if the process is to continue. The problems of production and consumption are interwoven in this model: Money channeled into investments detracts from consumption. With increased incomes, consumption also increases; this tends to deter money from investments. Productive capacity must therefore be regulated, if not by the free market and entrepreneurial activity, then by government intervention in the form of monetary and fiscal policies—clearly a Keynesian proposal incorporated within the model to keep it on an even a keel as possible.

This model can clearly be seen to apply to the developed and the developing countries both, since it is of such scope that its principles apply to both types of economies providing that its parameters are adjusted so that the natural and warranted rates of growth tend to equality, that is, so long as the potential and actual growth rates deviate little, if at all.

This model is a mixture of classical macroeconomics and Keynesian economics. The Keynesian influence is seen by the requirement of government to act as a regulator of the economy, maintaining sufficient investment and consumption levels whenever these fall short of, or exceed, the amount sufficient to maintain the system's functioning within growth orientation. The classical influence is seen in its very emphasis on equilibrium, striving to equate aggregate demand with aggregate supply. As labor produces and consumes and as aggregate savings in the form of investments retool industry and restock inventories, these producers as consumers have money available for consumption equal to $l - s$, which is the marginal propensity to consume.

When this equals aggregate supply, then aggregate demand and aggregate supply are in equilibrium, which is indeed a Say-like condition. Through the actions taken by businesspeople and the government, a set rate of economic growth can be planned and achieved according to the claims of this model, with the risks of overproduction and underconsumption or excess inflation or deflation curtailed. In the Harrod-Domar model, therefore, a post-Keynesian formulation is stated in which the classical Law of Markets has a definitive and positive role.

MARRIS ON MANAGERIAL CAPITALISM

While economists such as Harrod and Domar were concerned with the problems of the macro economy in light of the trauma of the Great Depression, a different approach to the postwar economy was taken by economists who sought to analyze and understand the dynamics of the corporation as it came to be and developed after the war. The resources of wartime were converted to peacetime production, and this required the techniques developed for waging war to be transformed to peaceful uses. Computers, which provided new possibilities with increasingly sophisticated program techniques and memory banks, together with the necessity for the demobilized men to make up for "lost time," opened new vistas for consumption and production. This required industrial reorganization for providing the most efficient forms of exploitation of resources at the lowest aggregate total costs while yielding the highest possible profit margins.

This was a period in which both conformity and individuality were stressed. It was an era of organization men, of standardization in production and in thought, in which the conformity of military life was transformed into the working patterns of the lower levels and middle management. It was an era of individuality and uniqueness, where the innovative commercial attitude was needed to break into new markets and exploit to the limit the existing ones. Thus, one of the most important skills of upper management was to take into account this dualistic conformity-individuality, to mold them and work with them in a manner that would open new markets, provide profit levels that would allow refinancing, and ensure employment and growth. The new economic system that subsequently rose from the ashes of World War II and that resulted in the reorganization and rehabilitation of industry is managerial capitalism—a system of which Robin Marris is one of the important theoreticians.

While this system is unique to the postwar era, its tenets are steeped in Say's Law of Markets, as demonstrated in the argument to follow.

Marris's work analyzes the corporation as it has developed in the post-war environment, and it is in this micro situation of the firm that concepts of supply and demand do not reach macro proportions. Hence, while Say's Law is a macro concept, it is necessary to analyze Marris's theory to demonstrate how the Law of Markets can nevertheless be derived, for he constructed this theory to treat the big corporation.

Marris delineates his area of discussion to the economic systems of North America and Western Europe in the mid-twentieth century, in which the means of production are concentrated in the large joint-stock companies. He explains that

> in many sectors of economic activity the classical entrepreneur has virtually disappeared. His role was essentially active and unitary; once dismembered, no devise of collective abstraction could put him together again. As a result . . . entrepreneurship in the modern corporation has been taken over by transcendent management, whose function differs in kind from those of the traditional subordinate or "mere manager." These people, it is argued, can wield considerable power without necessarily holding equity, sharing profits or carrying risks.[4]

He states that this form of capitalism did not result from a managerial revolution but from the transition for the traditional forms of capitalism evolving into the giant conglomerates, where the division and specialization of labor necessitates a specific class of people to define market areas, provide programs of production, and establish production guidelines.

Traditional economics can therefore be contrasted with managerial capitalism, for traditional economics assumes that the decision maker has property rights over his capital, rights that are restricted by what the markets are able to handle and by the law that proscribes the extent upon which other people and their positions can be infringed. Furthermore, traditional (Marshallian) economics dictates that if the decision maker's behavior is such that his business operates at a loss, a point will be reached where he will have to close down production.

In the era of managerial capitalism these conditions are not binding. Corporate managers are legally obligated to their shareholders, but the extent of this obligation has not been clearly defined, especially for conflicts of personal or corporate interests. Because of their size and product diversification, neither profit maximization nor breaking even is considered necessary for any specific product (a point challenged in this book); the inability to earn profits or to break even for any one product may be resolved by underwriting the loss through channeling the profits from other products. Marris suggests that profit maximization may indeed be relegated to secondary importance, superseded by the managers' seeking to maintain a good image for their corporations, so that policies of good labor relations and pollution control can be implemented. Whereas in classical and neoclassical theory the firms are sufficiently small that their policies have little or no effect on the positions of secondary, that is, supportive, industries, the firms of managerial corporation capitalism, whether acting as individual units or in concert, influence directly the policies and strategies of the secondary industries.[5]

The differences between the classical and neoclassical theories, on the one hand, and the theory of managerial capitalism, on the other, result in different approaches to demand and supply. In traditional economics, demand is considered monotonic and does not distinguish among the types of consumers but merely among the types of products, their production costs, and their profitability; in managerial capitalism, demand is stimulated and exploited as well as directed toward the many nuances of consumer groups, both actual and potential. Supply in traditional economics is considered only in terms of output and its costs; in managerial capitalism, supply is related directly to financing. These points will be discussed shortly.

In his approach to managerial capitalism, Marris discusses the firm and its relationship to the markets it generates. First to be considered is the firm's growth position and its maximum profit rate. The maximum growth rate of the firm is expressed by the following equation:

$C^{*}\bullet \; = p\,(l - i/p \bullet \bar{g}) \,/\, (l - \bar{g})$, where

$C^{*}\bullet$ is the maximum financially permitted growth rate

p is the parameter of return after deducting taxes and entrepreneur's (that is, manager's) subsistence

i is the average interest rate on debts

$\bar{g}$ is the maximum-permitted leverage (gearing) ratio, that is, the ratio of money borrowed to the money reinvested in the capital structure.

Where p is the profit rate after tax deductions and manager's wages, the optimum rate of profit given the firm's maximum growth rate is as follows:

$p^{*} \; = [l/(l/f_C + a_S/f_D\,] + (\beta_S \bullet v/a_S \bullet f_D/f_C)$, where

p^{*} is the optimum growth rate and is associated with the maximum growth rate

f_C is the reciprocal of the capital-output ratio, itself a function of d, the symbol for the diversification rate on which growth depends

a_S is an adjustable parameter representing, the slope of the supply-growth function, determined by the firm's existing money supply

f_D is the function which represents the growth of demand for the firm's output with respect to diversification

β_S is the stock market's influence on the firm's activity. Although not related directly to the demand for the firm's products, it is related indirectly as market conditions result in, and are reflected by, the firm's diversification programs

v is the constrained valuation ratio, that is, the ratio of the market value to the net assets, constrained by being held constant.

The values v, f_C and f_D make their appearances in other equations, namely, $C^{*}\bullet = (f_C/f_D \bullet \delta D^{*}/\delta C^{*}\bullet) \div (l + \delta D^{*}/\delta C^{*}\bullet)$, with f_C and f_D retaining their values and the expression

$\delta D\bullet/\delta C^{*}\bullet$ equal to $(l - m) \bullet f'_D/m \bullet f'_C$,

with m being the profit margin as affected by policy decisions; the primed values are changes in the ratio of capital to output and in the growth of demand for the firm's output with regard to diversification, respectively. The value of c in the equation $C^{*}\bullet = am/c - \beta v$ is determined by the equation $c = c(d)$, expressing the capital-output ratio as a function of diversification, with the ratio f_C/f_D being a highly sensitive function of diversification. Further, $D\bullet = D(d,m)$, $C\bullet = D\bullet$, with $C^{*}\bullet = D\bullet$. The conclusion is that $C^{*}\bullet$, which is the maximum financially permitted growth rate, dependent on net profits after deduction of the entrepreneur-manager's costs and net interest on debts—and considering that the gearing ratio is equal to the relationship between diversification and profits—$C^{*}\bullet$ is the maximum growth rate permitted by finance for both production and diversification as assessed by p^{*}, the optimum growth rate. Since $C^{*}\bullet$ depends on the demand for diversified output with prices set in accordance with the profit margin, this is another way of stating Say's Law—that output generates consumption.

Demand, for Marris's theory, consists of two subclasses. In one are the pioneers who experiment with products without being influenced by others in their experimentation; in the other are the sheeplike consumers who try a product on the recommendation of others or because they have become acquainted with the product through association with other people and their purchasing patterns. The aggregate demand function for product *i* therefore takes the form $Qi = N_p \cdot \phi_p + N_a \cdot \phi_s$, where N_p is the number of pioneers, N_a is the number of active consumers, and the functionals ϕ_p and ϕ_s represent the pioneer and sheeplike demand curves. Aggregate demand for the group of consumers for product *i* must meet one of these three conditions: (1) gestation, where $N_a = 0$, so that $Qi = N_p \cdot \phi_p$; (2) saturation, in which $N_a = N_s$ and $Qi = N_s \cdot \phi_s$; and (3) the explosion stage, where there exist instability and fluctuation between gestation and saturation. With regard to a product's profitability, Marris states that without diversification all the firm's products reach saturation, with their profits being determined by the economic conditions of the latter stages of their market lives. These stages are likely to be less favorable than during their early stages because with the passing of time their consumers are more aware of both the products and their competitors, with the general decline of the products' utilities as the consequence. Marris maintains that

> in fact we may reasonably view the profitability of a product over the whole history of gestation, explosion and saturation as consisting of an early rise followed by a flattening, then gradual, possibly asymptotic, decline. . . . the average profit contribution of young or youngish products must always exceed that of old products, and the higher the proportion of moderately young products in the catalogue at any given time, the higher, other things being equal, the average rate of return. This effect, which is possibly associated with the diversification rate, must be set against the negative effect of declining intrinsic utility. We may then suppose that at moderate rates of diversification, the average rate of return *increases* with the rate of diversification, then, as declining intrinsic utility sets in and becomes increasingly severe, the position is reversed. This is probably what is implied when business men say that diversification may sometimes enhance profitability.[6]

Hence the decline in profits results in production cutbacks. This reduction in profits is brought about by rising costs and a decline in demand due to competition among producers' goods. $C^* \cdot$ and $D \cdot$, when equal, means that a decline in $D \cdot$ must, under static conditions, that is, where a single product is involved, bring about a decline in $C^* \cdot$.

The supply side of this equation is geared for maximum growth and is dependent on the stock market as well as on managerial responses to production and demand conditions. Another way in which Marris states the maximum growth position is $C^{*}\bullet \triangleq a - p - \beta v$, with p substituting for $\bar{g}$, which is the leverage or gearing ratio. Significant for this approximation is the retention ratio, symbolized by the letter r, which is the ratio of retained earnings to gross earnings—earnings being profits less debt interest, with dividends on preferred shares included as debt, and retained earnings being gross earnings less dividends on ordinary stock, with all other shares not included as debt. The retention ratio thus defines profits, a definition necessary when the total picture of the firm's growth position is considered. The coefficients in the approximation statement a and β are rigorously delineated by the firm's existing money supply, and the stock market's impact on the firm is fairly determinate; this statement becomes a close approximation when the uncertainty of the coefficients is reduced, thus allowing the managers to act with relative certainty in accordance with the firm's capabilities in output and within the confines of the stock market.

The net profits delineated by the retention ratio allow the managers to plan further diversification and therefore seek capital for additional financing. Investments allow the firm greater degrees of freedom for further diversification and higher output targets. The newer products planned tend to greater sales over the existing and established products, which have already been marketed over time and which confront competition with the products of other firms; therefore, the greater the sales of these new products, the greater the profits yielded by the firm. If the firm's past experience has resulted in financial success, then its present drive for capital accumulation, other things being equal, will also be successful. The greater the production output and the wider the range of diversification, the higher the sales, with a possibly higher retention ratio; but this depends on the current managerial strategy.

FURTHER REMARKS

Marris's argument is that because the firm's growth is determined by its money supply and its showing on the stock market and because the firm's money supply is determined by profits and debts as the stock market makes its impact on the firm with respect to the firm's position in competition and its ability to attract consumption for its products, the firm's supply is related directly to its demand position. Thus, for the microeconomic situation of the firm, Marris, perhaps unwittingly, has reestablished a Say-like condition in the mechanics of his managerial supply-and-demand concepts. In the macro sense Marris advocates equilibrium, be it static or dynamic, to the alternative of disequilibrium. He states that if the vertical segment of the valuation curve—which represents the ratio of the market value to net assets and replaces the ratio of return as the variable dependent on the growth rate of the firm—can correspond to the inflexible growth rate, then the firm will be in dynamic equilibrium. He maintains that if not, then chronic disequilibrium, or at least the failure of the ideal conditions of ensuring economic health—the "Golden Age" conditions—will not be met.[7] This is a projection of the composition of the aggregate firm on the economy, with each firm maintaining dynamic equilibrium and by inference, the entire economy in a condition of growth as determined by the total of the firm's output and the total consumption. In other words, so long as diversification ensures a greater range of products in competition, these products, through marketing and sheeplike behavior, will be sold, thereby maintaining the economy in a state of equilibrium and growth, *ergo*, Say's Law of Markets in managerial-entrepreneurial clothing.

Thus, with managerial economics as interpreted by Marris and with the Harrod-Domar model, the situation remains as Keynes stated: Say's Law, brought into question during the Great Depression, has been shown to be durable enough to withstand all subsequent onslaughts; it has been incorporated into contemporary theory in the guise of equilibrium, be it static or dynamic. This is so to the extent that it has become almost axiomatic in economic reasoning that the best economic system is one in which supply is consumed *in toto*, with demand being of sufficient strength to move all existing goods and services to make room for further production.

The hard world of the dismal science of economics nevertheless remains removed from the esoteric theories of its practitioners. The axiom of equilibrium falls by the wayside when challenged by the contemporary problems of stagnating production and unemployment and inflation levels that threaten the very social fabric in which the economic systems operate. Yet, the only valid way to understand and treat contemporary economic circumstances is to place them within a theoretical framework and draw out their consequences. This theoretical framework must, however, relate to the real world as much as abstraction allows. This requires that no equilibrium be the basis for theory, but that it be dynamic disequilibrium, in which new products enter the markets while others are phased out, while the money supply and general liquidity depend on the proposed utilities of investments and aggregate utility functions for production and consumption. Most certainly within the confines of the Harrod-Domar model growth can be achieved in a nonvolatile manner, which was necessary in the aftermath of the Great Depression and World War II. The diseconomies of the depression and the necessity to cope with the war certainly required economic policies by fiat. This is in keeping with Keynesian theory and has been shown to be inoperable in the postwar years as industry developed to meet existing demand and to stimulate further demand. Marris most certainly shed light on the contemporary firm's inner dynamics; but when relating the firm to the macro economy, he is guilty of reinstating Say's Law, albeit in more esoteric terms than used by its originator.

In the chapters to follow a theory is developed that considers the firm in contemporary economics as a micro element within the macro setting; the macro economy is treated with respect to the dynamics of the firm, establishing disequilibrium patterns and market shifts. This theory is discussed in terms of international commerce and the developing countries.

The world's economies are in recession; perhaps the treatment of the business cycle with respect to dynamic disequilibrium, presented in these pages, will be of assistance in understanding our contemporary situation and will provide possible suggestions for alleviating the crisis.

PART II
THE ECONOMICS OF THE CONTEMPORARY FIRM

3

COMMENTS ON THE THEORETICAL AND INSTITUTIONAL BASIS

> At the center of the economist's stage is the market, with its wheeling and dealing, and its central act in which two parties make an exchange because each prefers what he gets to what he gives in return. That act of exchanging is the source and proof of all economic gain, which explains the economist's preoccupation with it. Yet market exchange is neither necessary nor sufficient for mutual gain. It is not necessary because innumerable exchanges occur without benefit of the market and because many unreciprocated acts also yield satisfaction to both giver and recipient. It is not sufficient because market exchanges often create not only satisfactions but also the needs they satisfy, and anything that gives rise to both a need and its satisfaction is of little or no use to anyone.
>
> *Tibor Scitovsky,*
> *The Joyless Economy*

The contemporary firm shares with its neoclassical predecessor the intent to produce needs and wants by generating demand and to supply needs and wants through the manufacturing of appropriate goods and services. For both types of firm, diversification allows the continuing production until consumer preferences for all the firm's products reach a state of saturation and the market can no longer absorb further products. Diversification then ceases; and for the neoclassical firm, production is geared according to the movement of supplies, while for the contemporary firm, the steps to be taken depend on managerial strategy.

In an article on management and linear programming, A. Charnes and W. W. Cooper described contemporary management activity as being threefold. First is planning, which involves considering various proposals raised by management and the assessing of all possible viable alternatives, including the metafunction of examining the procedures that ensure that all possible alternatives are stated. Second is the commitment of resources to those projects deemed profitable; this differs from planning because the potential resource allocation is a factor in project determination. This is therefore the operational stage and entails production. Third is management control to determine the extent to which the operations conform to the planning process and if not, whether changes have to be made in the plan or in production. Exact conformity, Charnes and Cooper maintain, is undesirable because it shows a lack of independence in planning and a lack of understanding of the problems in production when the project is executed.[1]

This list of managerial activity refers only to the application of the organizational aspects of management in the sense that it relates to the decision-making process with respect to proposed projects. Lacking in this list, among other points to be made later, is the first level of managerial activity, that of either innovation or imitation. Innovation and imitation are necessary aspects of managerial planning that take place prior to actual decision making and the commitment of resources. These are discussed in the chapters that follow.

It is also insufficient to list as the first step of management activity the consideration of various proposals toward decision making without taking into consideration the firm's position with respect to diversification, the gearing ratio indicating the firm's abilities to venture into new product areas, and the information that results from formulating proposals. The significance of this last point is that it provides the knowledge of current markets and possible development of new markets—knowledge that allows for the formulation of projects for innovation or imitation. Knowledge of existing and potential markets allows for the determination of the firm's abilities to enter into new markets or exploit the marketing trails set by other firms. It also registers an understanding of aggregate consumer liquidity with respect to the ability to absorb another imitating product and the potential willingness by consumers to direct a portion of their incomes toward a new product line. In both cases of innovation and imitation management must be ready to divert a portion of the firm's resources into products different from the present output. Such diversification of monetary and physical assets can be undertaken only when both the firm's internal position with respect to its markets and the actual and potential market responses are known and reasonably anticipated. The criterion of a successful market, for the actual and for the anticipated market, are the same: It is one that over a period of time, determined by the variability of consumers' responses, allows more firms to devote a greater part of their productive capacities toward exploitation of the market and thereby draw out its nuances. This continues until the aggregate diminishing returns on profits set in and reach the point where management considers the profit level unsatisfactory with respect to costs and possible market alternatives; this occurs when almost total market saturation is reached.[2] A dynamic managerial staff will assess this situation before it is reached and will begin drawing up plans for other products in different markets—markets that may have been established by entrepreneurial managers that are not yet formulated, hence representing a greater potential gamble with high profits if successfully entered.

The firms' operations and government policies for economic regulation have placed the economics of our time in a paradoxical situation. In practice, there is the macro position in which the total activities of the firms maintain the governing bodies as economic regulators that keep the economy in balance. When, for example, inflation exceeds the limits considered necessary for a healthy growth rate, the governing bodies act to curb the inflation through increased taxation and interest rates in order to reduce general liquidity. The printing presses are slowed to an allowable level set by the authorities to reduce the amount of money in circulation without bringing about severe deflation of the kind experienced in the Great Depression. Conversely, should the economy be moving toward a recession, steps are taken to reduce taxation and lower the interest rates, making greater liquidity available while watching the impact of greater money supplies from increased printing and the influence these policies have on stimulating greater production and competitive consumer prices. These policies seek to initiate the purchases of new capital equipment and the redeployment of labor in sectors where the marginal contribution is high. These policies are essentially Keynesian and meet the requirements of the Harrod-Domar model for achieving balanced and dynamic growth.

The managerial staffs of firms, however, operate from the vantage points their positions allow, and they have little or no concern for the macro situation other than its impact on their enterprises and decision-making possibilities. Since their markets cannot be determined precisely, they have a tendency to overproduce those goods that demonstrate success and accepted profit levels; this overproduction usually continues until competition from other firms reduces the level of profits and leads to near-market saturation. These policies are not macro oriented and are therefore not concerned with the Keynesian and Harrod-Domar dynamics. These micro policies are based on the techniques of production and market exploitation and fall outside the scope of macro theory.

The paradox is that without macroeconomics the firms cannot thrive and without the aggregate contributions of the firms there could be no macro economy. Each approach operates independently of the other; yet they are inextricably involved. This involvement is historically based and from its history the paradox of macro- and microeconomics developed.

During the pre-Great Depression times industry's operation according to the profit ethos was constrained by only a very passive government role in the economy. Previous recessions and depressions were allowed to run their full lengths with little government interference or counteractivity. Because in retrospect industry was not complex in its scope and operations, economic slowdowns, as severe and enduring as they were, did not bring about such extensive damage that they could not be overcome with the replenishment of stocks and with new markets. Recovery always followed, no matter how intense the depressions; living standards were rising, and in spite of the cyclical fluctuations that brought about diseconomies, faith in the system remained undaunted by the majority. Marxism and other socialist fringes consequently made little impact on the working populations of the capitalist economies.

It was after World War I that the capitalist system faced its greatest challenge. The world was recovering from the most intensive and bloodiest war in history, with its conclusion followed by utopian promises for world unity and peace. The costs of that war have yet to be determined in terms of the future. One cost, however, was industry's inability to absorb demobilized men; this, in spite of the increased demand these people generated on industrial production. The consequence was a depression.

As with all depressions, this one led to recovery as the soldiers were eventually absorbed into industry. Those who saw battle acquired a maturity far beyond their years. Together with the refugees from the war-torn countries, they brought the skills necessary for rebuilding the societies whose economic structures were previously geared for turning out instruments of destruction. Industry, employing these men to increase production, acted not out of benevolence but out of its own self-interests. Recovery was underway and money was flowing into the stock and commodities markets. This rate of flow represented a newly found confidence in the economic system that was backed by the prospects of world peace as established and guided by the League of Nations.

Industrial output was regulated by the markets' abilities to absorb the products and by the marginal utility of consumption according to the workers' fixed incomes. This was not so with the paper markets: Stocks and bonds were being sold and bought at rates that grew to have no bearing on the worth of those who floated the issues. The markets went out of control, with the paper value of shares increasing while industrial output followed behind, increasing at decreasing rates. When the differential between the paper shares and the industrial base to support these shares became too great, there was rapid deflation, with great monetary losses. The consequence was the Great Depression, with industry at a near-standstill, accompanied by mass unemployment.

In hindsight, it appears ironic that the great potential output of industry remained idle. People were seeking employment, but industry, lying idle and unused, was unable to provide work. Still, in light of the rapid deflation that led to the crash, the lessons were learned. No longer were the stock markets to be left for speculation without proper controls. Government intervention in market activities in the form of exchange commissions were established to prevent worthless shares being dumped on the markets, and regulations were set down to determine what shares could be issued, how many of these shares could be offered for sale, and who the buyers could be. Monopolies, oligopolies, and other practices that hinder competition served as material for the trustbusters and fair-practice regulating authorities. Government-sponsored works programs were initiated to provide employment with the ultimate objective of generating demand through increased purchasing power. It was considered that this new money flowing into the economy would result in industry's reemploying workers to meet the demand. This is Keynesian reasoning, with the purpose of establishing a working supply-and-demand relationship; bringing the economy to a viable level of output; and through demand, eliminating rapid deflation and inflation.

Keynesian practices were disrupted by World War II, fought to resolve the issues remaining from the first world conflict. There is little doubt that had there been no other war, Keynesian policies would have moved the world out of its depression. For this reason and for historical reasons pertaining to the development of economic thought, governments adapted their macroeconomic policies on grounds similar to the recommendations of Keynesian theory and the Harrod-Domar model. The emphasis was on eliminating all volatile action, maintaining equilibrium yet allowing the economies to expand at rates that tended to guarantee fairly stable rates of growth. A new confidence was inspired in the economies, and the growth rates set by industry and government were based on the abilities of the economies to meet the challenges of the new demand after the demobilization of troops left a new working and consuming force to be absorbed into industry. In this sense, the mistakes of the aftermath of the first world conflict were corrected and growth targets set because of the new working and consuming force were largely met.

As safe as equilibrium growth seemed, however, it could not work for long. The firms that evolved after World War II, as well as those already established before the war, were not able to remain within a macroeconomic policy based on dynamic equilibrium. Their operations became such that through competition and market building, as well as through phasing out of products and elimination of nonlucrative markets, a dynamic system was set into motion; but it was one that was nonequilibrium oriented. Those firms that prospered did so by demonstrating flexibility and innovation as well as the ability to move into a market already pioneered and profitable. Industry thus acquired a built-in disequilibrium, moving into markets that showed a profit margin deemed respectable by its managerial boards and phasing out those markets that were unprofitable. Costs came to be calculated in terms of future profits and present programs. The tenets of neoclassical equilibrium, of producing until marginal costs equal marginal revenue, were tossed aside with the object of entering new markets and producing until management determines that allocating the terms of production along other lines can be more profitable. Because industry generates economic growth through production and by providing employment for consumption, and because the government acting as regulator of the macro economy has not been able to find an equilibrium pattern to impose on this disequilibrium situation, an *ad hoc* combination of monetary and fiscal policies has become the standard macro tool for regulating the economy, maintaining it on a more-or-less even keel and therefore regulating growth.

The difficulty was then, and remains so today, that the prime objective of the firms is profits. Because of this new markets are opened and if successful innovative profits are reaped, markets are maintained in which profits fluctuate only marginally and firms move into markets where innovation has already set the demand patterns, provided that necessary retooling costs are such that the net profit yield is high.

The macro approach is different because although each firm must treat its own position with respect to its established and potential markets, the government must consider the economy *in toto* as it responds and reacts to the individual firm's policies when put into action. What is beneficial for the macro economy may therefore be stifling for individual firms and such macro policies may cause disruptions in production, shrinking markets, and unemployment—which is a symptom of such policies.

Marketing and production techniques have become increasingly sophisticated. At the same time, the consuming public has become more attuned to product differentiation and quality. Given these developments, the question is, why haven't macro techniques and conceptions progressed as well? The answer is that echoes of the Great Depression still rebound, and they influence directly the decision-making processes of the respective government agencies responsible for overseeing the macro economy. The macro techniques are countercyclical, seeking to maintain equilibrium;[3] this is so in spite of the engines of economic growth, the firms and corporations which produce, market, and therefore employ, operate according to the disequilibrium conditions of the markets. The government's conceptual basis for economic operations is Keynesian-cum-Harrod-Domar, and macro equilibrium policies cannot relate to the overall disequilibrium generated by the dynamic disequilibrium of the firms.

There can indeed be no economic growth when macro production and investments are held in equilibrium as a result of government policies. Under these circumstances industry can respond only to *ad hoc* measures taken by government authorities. The ultimate consequence is that the degrees of freedom in managerial decision making are severely limited by government policies; with all good intentions of seeking a stable growth pattern, the result is the determination of the guidelines by which industry can operate and expand. The problem for contemporary industrial and postindustrial economics is that as ever-increasing sophisticated and cost-saving methods of production are being employed, with the efficiency of labor correspondingly increasing, government authorities are treating the economy as if another worldwide and severe depression is approaching. By stifling disequilibrium by way of equilibrium policies, the government does not allow the markets to function effectively in clearing supplies and bringing new firms into competition while allowing those firms whose profits have been reduced or whose managers choose to direct their funds into other projects, to withdraw. Thus, although there is unemployment and inflation—conditions that have existed since the Industrial Revolution—these are treated by the monetary and fiscal policies in agreement with Keynesian theory and the equilibrium-oriented Harrod-Domar model. The medicine is inappropriate, and its administrators look with puzzlement as the economy fails to respond.

This paradoxical situation is found not only in macro theory. Marris, as an exponent of managerial capitalism, in his chapter "Possible Macro Implications," supports equilibrium growth.

> The answer [to the question of determining the rate at which technology is endogenous to equilibrium] is that we know that steady growth requires the diversification rate and associated growth rate to satisfy two conditions: the growth rate of real output and hence purchasing power must be equal to the natural rate, which is in turn *determined* by the diversification rate, but every growth rate also "requires" a certain diversification rate in order to maintain stability in the consumption function. Therefore the growth rate and diversification rate must be such that the diversification rate is equal to the rate "required" by the growth rate, and that the growth rate is, in turn, the result of technical progress at the rate consistent with the diversification rate. We call such a growth rate a *quasi-natural* rate, and the associated diversification rate a quasi-natural diversification rate. We do not ask how an economy may find such a rate, but do insist that it is a valid requirement of economic growth. Its reality may be seen in recent economy in the United States, where there is considerable evidence that because the condition has not or cannot be met, consumers are increasingly reluctant to maintain consumption demand at the level required by the productive rate of progress.
>
> It is thus perfectly possible that an economy may reach a situation where, until some major industrial or socio-economic revolution occurs, no quasi-natural rate exists. Disequilibrium states will then become chronic. This is one way, in fact, of explaining the post-Keynesian condition of "secular stagnation." But it also seems possible that, under other circumstances, there may exist within limits a continuous range of growth rates, all of which are quasi-natural. Within the range, small changes in the diversification rate will always generate changes in the rate of technical progress which were precisely consistent with change in the growth rate of demand for which the new diversification rate was the required rate. Productive innovations would have the qualitative characteristics necessary for consumers always to want to exploit them to the full.[4]

Marris's equation of the diversification rate as determined by the technical actualities and possibilities with the so-called quasi-natural rate of growth is somewhat puzzling in light of his condemnation of disequilibrium because equilibrium is inconsistent with diversification. Moreover, not only in the United States but in all industrialized (or technetronic) countries, production must be geared to the levels of potential and actual consumption—which of course does not mean that such production will be consumed, hence portraying the failure of Say's Law in Marris's interpretation. The notions of natural and quasi-natural growth rates are derived from the Harrod-Domar model, in which growth rates are associated with the *present* technology and the state of the arts, which allow for production to expand according to the means of production and the measured effective demand. Innovation in the immediate future is not considered, even though innovation can alter the technologies and affect the markets and demand schedules in a dynamic manner.

Furthermore, Marris fails to explain how managers can enter into new markets and phase out old ones within an equilibrium framework. The mustering of capital, the retooling and restructuring of productive plant, and innovation and imitation do not occur within a balanced industrial program. Should management work strictly within the limits of its available capital, no matter how the gearing ratio is computed, there would be little market formation, little imitation, and only an insignificant and extremely marginal amount of innovation. Indeed, such near-stagnation and restricted market formation violates the very notion of the gearing ratio, which Marris defined as the ratio of the money borrowed to the amount of money reinvested in the capital structure; money borrowed for investment must be directed to sources other than current production, for the profits from this production must be such that costs are covered. If not, then the losses in production would bring about a closure of the line of merchandise produced. Investments must therefore be geared toward new products, and such new production is a disruption of equilibrium, of the *status quo* in production. It is significant that Marris noted that the quasi-natural rate of growth is not maintained in the United States and that consumers are increasingly reluctant to maintain consumption demand at the level required by the productive rate of progress. The U.S. consumer is not shaped in his consumption patterns by Say's Law, no matter how esoteric its statement. Neither is the consuming public in the other industrial and postindustrial technetronic societies shaped by Say's Law. It can therefore be assumed that in his chapter cited above, had Marris taken his theory to its macro implications instead of leaving it on the sidelines, he would have revised his treatment of macroeconomics and its implications on his micro usage and theory.

It is somewhat paradoxical, therefore, that in light of the necessity for diversification and the absence of equilibrium within the major industrial firms, both macro and micro economists continue to stress the importance of equilibrium as if the economy can be understood in the same way as an accountant's balance sheet. This is due to the persistent influence of Say's Law. That governments must regularly revise their monetary and fiscal programs and projections to attempt to cope with the changing economic picture indicates on the macro level that there are no "built-in" regulators maintaining the economy in equilibrium, neither static nor dynamic. Marris stresses the entrance into imitative markets, the necessity for innovation, the phasing out of those products that no longer yield profits, and the releasing of resources for different production lines; yet, he argues for equilibrium, which is surely a contradiction. The decline in profitability is due to the changes in the tastes and preferences of consumers as well as to the response to the variations in purchasing power of the currency with respect to the availability of closely competing products at lower prices. Marris referred to the United States as an economy that has not or cannot find the quasi-natural growth rate; he failed to draw the proper conclusion that the macro equilibrium that he advocates does not exist in the United States economy because dynamic disequilibrium allows for changing tastes and preferences, consumptions of close competitors, and fluctuations in the dollar's purchasing power, which often account for revisions in consumers' allocations of their liquidity and consumption schedules. The reluctance of consumers to maintain demand "at the level required for the productive rate of progress" is largely because of the firms' dynamics, in which new products are introduced and others phased out, with pricing in accordance with the currency's purchasing power, itself determined by the competitive choice of products vying for consumer demand. The productive rate of progress is therefore nonexistent, nor can it exist in a dynamic disequilibrium setting in a capitalist framework. On both the macro and micro levels, so long as dynamic equilibrium is maintained as the objective, there will be no resolution of this paradox. It is necessary, therefore, to discuss the firm and the macro economy in terms of disequilibrium. The next chapter considers the firm's policies and discusses its relationship to the forces of macro disequilibrium.

4

ON DECISION MAKING AND THE THEORY OF VALUE

ON UTILITY AND ENTROPY

Decisions are made on the basis of information. When the information is detailed, the decision is made with assurance; when the information is scanty, the decision is taken on less firm ground. Information concerning the same problem and the same set of alternative choices may be available in greater detail for one person than for another. The probability of making the better decision is greater when the information content is more complete than when the information is less detailed. Nevertheless, no ironclad guarantee assures that the person with the greater information available will necessarily make the wiser choice.

Economic decision making is necessary for the consumer who needs to allocate liquidity between such alternatives as consumption and saving, as well as for the manager who must decide what programs to undertake and how best to allocate available liquidity for present and future projects, as well as deciding which already-existing projects should be encouraged, which of them should be phased out, and what production techniques should be used to cut costs and increase output. Consumers, for example, will shun a product they know is not of their liking or is faulty in their opinion, or they will shun a product if their information about the product is negative because of experiences related by friends and acquaintances. The manager who has researched a potential project in all its possible nuances has a better chance of obtaining marketability than the manager who plans production after taking a cursory view of the potential marketability and production techniques. The more complete the information, the greater and more rigorous the understanding of the investment and the opportunities. Similarly, a speculator in the stock market who has a fine understanding of the workings of the market, or who has an "inside tip" about the declaration of dividends for a share, has the advantage in the decision-making process over the novice or ill-informed speculator who operates only on the basis of "gut feelings" when playing the markets.

The condition and quality of information available to the decision maker—whether acting as consumer, investor, or speculator—depends on the objective situation of the market or product. The utility of this information depends, however, on the content and quality of the information available *and* the subjective interpretation of this information. Hence, information that is consistent and complete for $n > 1$ decision makers has possible differing utilities, especially so because no two persons have identical utility schedules. This is the case when, *a priori*, two experienced consumers have identical information but prefer different competing products. Also, two sophisticated investors may act differently on the same "tip," each according to an individual utility schedule. With regard to disseminating information, managers know that advertising must be broad enough to reach a wide audience yet narrow enough to extol the product's qualities in order to capture the largest audience of the specific type of consumer and to interest potential consumers not specifically considered in the original market planning. It is in this context of objective and subjective duality that information, utility, and disutility, which is entropy, must be treated.

Joel Demski has written that information "refers to data that may alter a decision maker's predictions."[1] In addition, information consists of data meaningful only to those who receive and comprehend it. To a person who has no training in physics, the statement that an atomic particle can be plotted in a gas chamber with regard to movement or can be identified with respect to position, but not both, is a piece of data most certainly; for this person, however, this piece of data is without meaning, lacking in relevance. To a person who is tone deaf, new approaches to harmonics are data that have no significance. The data must have content presented and must be relevant to those who receive the information for it to be of utility.

For this discussion, the data have to do with economics and the recipient is the decision maker, whether the consumer, the manager, or the investor. These data on economics meet the requirement stated by Demski in that they may alter the decision maker's predictions and affect the decision maker's actions. This information can be accepted in its entirety or in part; it may also be rejected in its entirety or in part, depending on the decision maker's interpretation of the information and his objectives.

For this discussion, an information system is defined as a body of relevant data that may be either total in content or partially complete. This means that two kinds of information systems exist: a closed information system and an open information system. The closed information system is complete in content, containing all the relevant data; any further data that might be added are redundant. This system is consistent in the sense that no contradictions and no ambiguities are involved. For example, on a certain day a transaction occurs in which a specific sum of money is exchanged between two identified individuals representing two specified firms; they thereby conclude a production and marketing merger. Investors who have access to this information can determine the utility of investing in the merged firms; the people involved in the transaction can formulate their business strategies before and after the transaction is completed; and consumers, when confronted with the product through advertising, can determine whether to place their liquidity on the product.

This closed information system is bounded by a time-signature and is isolated from the influence of data that could otherwise alter its contents. The utility of the system, however, varies from one receiver to another. For the information system $A_t = [a_1, a_2, \cdots, a_n]$, where A_t is the statement *in toto* and $a_1, a_2, \cdots, a_n$ are the individual statements that compose the system. The utility is assessed by setting the statement within the maximum and minimum boundaries, so that $0 < a_t < 1$, meaning that the information system having relevance for a certain time has a utility rating between the limits of maximum utility and complete entropy.

The assessment of the utility depends on individual preferences and the probabilities of these preferences for the decision maker. Those individuals considering such a system must therefore relate it to their own decision making schedule. In the preceding example, for instance, the decision maker may be acquainted with the people involved in the transaction and the type of product that will result from the agreement. Although the decision makers do not doubt the content of the information, they may be sceptical about the agreement yielding a marketably viable item, their scepticism based on their background knowledge of the firms and their representatives. They may therefore rate the probabilities of each of the information statements as being somewhat low, indicating that the transaction will not be economically viable when production and marketing begin. He may rate the entire system low or rate some of its elements low, thus himself assigning a low utility rate for the system. Another person may have a different opinion, also know the people involved in the transaction, and have high regard for the two firms. He may assign a high utility rate to the transaction *in toto* and therefore accept for himself a high utility rate for the deal, placing his liquidity at the newly formed company's disposal.[2] Whether the information has high or low utility is thus strictly subjective, depending on the individual's interpretation and the significance this information holds for him. This system is closed and noncontradictory because no further information has relevance to that contained within the system. Because the structure of the information is such that contradictory statements are excluded and because this information is restricted in content—bound by the time-signature indicating the duration of its relevance—this system is both consistent and complete.

An incomplete information system is one in which one or both types of conditions occur: Either the system has been "infiltrated" by information elements of other systems or there is insufficient data within the system itself to reduce or eliminate the uncertainty concerning the validity and utility of the information necessary to make a certain decision. Since the system is open, it is by definition a system that is incomplete and therefore not subject to the restriction of a bounded time-signature. It may thus contain elements from other information systems that influence its general validity.

Consider the system A in which are incorporated the elements b_1, b_2, c_3, and c_4 of information systems B and C (it is of no significance whether B and C are open or closed). Such an information system exists for a firm prior to the finance minister's announcement of the proposed annual budget, when the investor's decision to place his money at the firm's disposal must not only take into consideration the firm's present position but also the effects the budget may have in the near future, after its announcement. This information consists of factual statements and speculation, the facts gathered from the departmental bargaining and "in-fighting" for a larger portion of the budgetary cake and the speculation gathered from circulating rumors, some of which may be fact and none of which can be substantiated before the announcement. The firm's information system is A-closed; yet as the budget dateline approaches, the firm's information system becomes open, infiltrated by elements of other systems, elements such as the positions of other firms and the economy's present viability and projected responses after the budgetary address.

Nor is there any certainty that an information system, once opened, will become closed again. In this example, the instability brought about in the economy because of the budget's impact may be such that new information must be incorporated into A at irregular intervals as the firm seeks to adjust to the changing circumstances. An open system is subject to the incorporation of conflicting information statements, such as differing predictions among economic analysts as to the firm's short-run viability during the period of adjustment. The firm's managers and the investor are thus confronted with an open-ended information system that contains a degree of uncertainty expressed by the utilities of the information statements as they respond to the new conditions and by the utilities of the newly incorporated statements as they are considered on their merits and their impacts on system A in general.

An open system is one, therefore, in which insufficient data exist for eliminating or even reducing significantly the uncertainty in the decision-making process, although a degree of reduction can be achieved over time with proper research. A manager has developed an information system P_t concerning the viability of a new product he is planning. Little information interference occurs in the production stages, and the level that does exist is taken into account by the system's parameters. The manager has undertaken extensive preliminary market surveys and computed the advertising and distribution costs. At this level the information system is closed and complete. In spite of all the groundwork, however, the information is insufficient for determining the product's viability over time after it has made its initial appearance. The level of competition and the price-cost ratios of competing firms cannot be measured, resulting in the inability to assess the product's longevity in the competitive market. Prior to the product's exposure to the market, the P_t system was closed and took the form $[p_1, p_2, \cdots, p_n]$, which in spite of the certainty and consistency of information at this time offered little certainty and would yield different information when the product reached the market.

In light of competition and unforeseen costs such as changes in distribution and advertising charges, P_t undergoes alteration, taking the form $P_{tn} \in [p_1, p_2, \cdots, p_m, \cdots, p_w \cdots]$, where the wth element in p is a statement contradictory to one of the other elements. This may pertain to the assessed utility of the product for a certain consuming populace in a specific socioeconomic neighborhood, or it may be a conflict between the expected profit rate for time t_m and the rate realized. All such deviations are not necessarily against the firm, however; the reality may be well above the manager's expectations and may thus result in his revision of the P system. The point is that the manager seeks to close the system as much as his reality allows him to; but the reality is a dynamic as expressed by shifts in his consuming public and the production, advertising, and distribution costs, which are changing. These changes throw the product into disequilibrium as opposed to P at time t before the product was placed on the markets and generated demand prior to imitative competition.

As the product's costs and profits fluctuate, so does the manager's information system. This system must be revised, always remaining behind the reality in its information content. The contradictions among those statements of P_t and P_{t_n} (P_{t_n} being more advanced in information content because of the product's market exposure and its ramifications) must be eliminated in the reformulation of P so that the manager and the firm's investors can obtain an accurate picture of the product's general position in order to assess its utility. Although the product's picture may be fairly accurate during the revised assessment after contradictions have been accounted for, that the product will maintain a steady course in its cost-profit ratio in the near future is not guaranteed. The product's utility rating for both the manager and investor depends, therefore, on the probability assessment of the product's prospects; and this assessment is based on the current P system, that is, on the information statements the system includes. The system is open ended because it remains outside human ability to predict the future with complete accuracy. Managers who determine that the product must be phased out because of its current poor performance may, upon revising the production preferences, find that their decision was an error in terms of profits, this based on the profitability of close competitors. Or the judgment to maintain the product during a current spell of high profits may be an error because of unstable markets and profit decline in the near future.

The decision maker's acceptance or rejection of a closed information system depends on his interpretation of the *probability* of the system *in toto*. Each statement depends on the others for its validity; and the system stands as a unit, consistent and complete. The system's probability depends on the probability of each of its elements, that is, the statements. In the preceding discussion of the closed system, the probability of both managers meeting on the prescribed date and signing the merger for the production of a good that has been thoroughly researched by representatives of both firms is, *ceteris paribus*, 100 percent; this is the objective probability and comes as a consistent and complete unit to the decision maker. The subjective probability, moreover, is just as significant for the decision maker. His understanding of the talents of the managers involved in the deal, his interpretation of their research abilities in general and specifically for the product in question, and his comprehension of the combined abilities of the firms to produce a viable product in terms of sales and profits—these are strictly subjective and formed as a result of experience and tastes. The probability assigned to this business arrangement is therefore subjective, although it considers the objective information of the closed system. The decision maker's utility preference for this agreement as a vehicle for investment takes the range between maximum utility, or 1, and complete disutility (entropy), or 0.

This utility assignment not only pertains to the investor but also to the managers involved in the agreement. Before the agreement is validated, the utility of the combined production has to be assessed by the firms' representatives. Given the same objective information that the investor receives, the managers of both firms have to assess the utility of their proposed agreement before it is validated. The reason for this is that before signing the agreement, the managers may propose other production alternatives; the utility of assigning resources in a bilateral association may thereby be relegated to a lower level of preference by one or both of the managers. Or the possibility may arise that current production problems require a reorientation of committed resources and techniques to salvage projects; this may require a delay in signing, which may bring the information to a state of low objective probability and hence entropy. Alternatively, a higher profit level than expected for current production may render the proposed information system a nonviable project because of the lack of economic necessity for merging with another firm. Thus, until the agreement is actually consummated, both managers must assess the utility from their perspectives to determine if the project is worthwhile.

The situation is more complicated with an open-ended information system. Not all the information is available, and that amount which one person may possess may not necessarily correspond to the exact amount understood by another. Hence, contradictions may exist, or the managers may include information that is not entirely relevant.

On the basis of this information, each decision maker must make his choice and act according to it. The probabilities each person assigns depend on the understanding each acquires, so that each decision maker thus removes the advantage of objectivity and becomes highly subjective, thereby increasing the risks of making erroneous decisions.

The decisions are made on the basis of expectations, of considering in the present the individualistically projected future results. Since these decisions are subjective—though there may be a general consensus as to what these expectations should be—the probabilistic assignment of values depends on individual preference schedules as determined by expectations. For one individual the probability of achieving a specific return on investment may be an inducement for placing his money, while for another the same or similar remuneration may be the factor that turns him against the investment because of his tax status. One person may have information that tells against the project while another person may have different information that provides incentives—with both pieces of information being in contradiction. One group of government advisers may advocate a tax increase during periods of stagnation and inflation as a means of encouraging people to reduce consumption when production is unable to meet effective demand, thereby withdrawing the pressures for price increases instead of increased production. Another group of advisers for the same government may press for a general tax reduction to stimulate effective demand, still further making it worthwhile for manufacturers to retool and resume production at levels that would absorb sufficient employment and rid the economy of stagnation.

As for the assessment of the probability, a statement that is part of given information is either true or false. Where the system is closed and no new information enters, the assessment is simple and the system's utility depends on the expectations of the decision makers involved. Where the system is open, the complications are almost limitless. Possessing only some of the statements, a decision maker can assess the validity of these statements by isolating the contradictions at his disposal and evaluating them according to the remaining information statements; he can thereby discard the offending statements. The difficulty arises later, when the statements he does not possess stand in contradiction with those he has already sanctioned. Another decision maker may possess the same set of statements as the first and be in possession of additional statements that allow him to discard the first set of statements as being untenable; yet, these are the very statements the other accepted as viable. Also, often probabilities are assigned on combinations of statements, for they provide fuller expression to expectations. Taken in combination, these statements may be accepted by some while rejected by others because their recombinations with still-different statements provide contradictions. Nevertheless, on the basis of available information each decision maker must make choices in keeping with expectations and assign utility schedules on this basis. The object of this assessment is to relate the information presented to the reality as it is understood, thereby reducing the subjective interpretation and increasing the component of reality in the judgment.

A way to minimize the difficulties of subjective assessment in decision making is to assign boundaries of verisimilitude according to expectations and allow these boundaries to represent the utilities on which the decisions are taken. With the upper boundary designated by 1 and the lower by 0, the upper limit indicates that a complete verisimilitude exists between the information system as it is available as a linguistic (or symbolic) structure describing a situation, so that the language relates directly to reality. The lower limit means that no relationship whatsoever exists between the language of the information system and the reality it purports to describe. For each decision maker, each information system lies between these boundaries and to the extent that the system moves between these limits, its position determines its utility and entropy. By so adapting this approach, the emphasis is shifted to the highly subjective interpretation and strong influence of personal expectations, to the analysis of the reality and the language used for dealing with reality.

For a closed system the determination of utility or entropy is an uncomplicated process. Because the system is free from all outside influences and hence experiences no change in content or ambiguity in meaning, the decision maker is confronted with a situation in which the information system either describes its reality accurately or it does not. The information system's time-signature states the period for which it is assumed to be valid, and this can be assessed with respect to the domain of reality to which the system relates. Because each statement, each element, within the system can be broken down into its components, these statements can be matched with that specific aspect of the reality domain to which each relates. On this basis each statement is subject to the determination of either utility or entropy; that is, either a statement relates to the reality for which it was constructed or it does not. After having derived a general consensus of each statement's validity—and as there are no contradicting statements or levels of ambiguity–the system can be taken *in toto* to be placed on a scale between 0 and 1. Its rating determines its objective status, and it is left to the decision maker to assess his personal utility with respect to this rating. His expectations may have brought him to considerations not allowed by the information system, and this approach may have led him to revise them; or his expectations may have been confirmed, but surely of firmer ground than before. In any case, the information system's utility (or lack of it) has been established with respect to the reality its language is intended to describe. The decision maker must then act on the basis of this knowledge.

The open-ended information system is more complicated than the closed system because contradictory statements may be raised and the information of other, not necessarily relevant, systems may be incorporated. Hence, the time-signature here takes on added significance, for it isolates the system within a time framework, making it controllable to a certain extent. Thus, the information system of A in time t_1 may or may not be equal in the quantity of statements and the import of their content to A_{t_2}; only an analysis of these systems can determine this. The problem is compounded by those statements existing in both time frames that may have different meanings because new statements that have been incorporated alter some of their nuances. Also, new statements may seem to be in accordance with the general direction of the information system yet upon close analysis may be contradictory. This situation requires the system be broken down and analyzed to determine which statements are necessary for the system's intention and which can therefore be removed without affecting its objective utility–a process that may entail breaking down individual sentences and restating them so that their troublesome parts can be removed.

For both the closed and open information systems, the utility in its objective form determines the extent to which the system presents a faithful description of reality. This is determined by the system's probability assessing its relation to reality. Probability is a function of the information content; it is represented by the letter I with the expression I/A_t representing the probability rating of A at the stated time t. I/A is a general expression for the probability of $A_A = \epsilon\ [P(A_t)]$, with $P(A_t)$ representing the probabilities of $a_1, \cdots, a_n$ statements within the information system. The utility of A_t is thereby assessed by focusing on each of the statements and determining the relationship to the reality for which they were formulated. This information system and its utility rating–between the limits of 0 and 1–is thus placed at the disposal of the decision maker as an objective perspective for consideration.

The probability of an open-ended information system's statements tends to vary over time, with A_{t_1} equaling or not equaling A_{t_2} in information content and objective utility. The utility of A, when open-ended, must be reexamined before decision makers act on the information at varying times. The difficulty of working with open systems is that the decision maker acts during a specific period of time with respect to the system's information, and this action requires that he treat the system as closed for the duration of the period in question. Nevertheless, the system is subject to fluctuations over the same time, rendering his subjective utility computations invalid, thereby entering a risk factor not accounted for in the period of time in which the decision is being considered and the act executed.

Such is the case, for example, with investing in shares. A firm presents itself as a dynamic organization, bringing diversified products into the markets, adjusting its production lines according to market needs, and using its excess capital for retooling and engaging in innovative and imitative projects. When becoming acquainted with the firm's internal situation—as defined by its prospectus—and with the information concerning its performance on the stock market, the investor has to decide if investing in the firm is sound. The total information at his disposal is incomplete because the system is open. At the same time, this information is bounded by a time-signature, so that the firm's share prices and potential profit taking cannot be determined for the future. In addition, there may be a new government policy that affects the direction of the firm's activities and the movement of its shares. Or, internal difficulties may bring about a reduction of the share prices and seriously affect the value of the shares. The bounded information is thus incomplete; nonetheless, such is the system within which the investor has to act. As the system changes, the investor must revise his calculations, each revision necessarily undertaken within a bounded information system whose content fluctuates. The time-signature is placed by the investor and his reality is in fluctuation.

The objective utility of an information system is determined by the probabilities of the system's statements as they relate to their domain and as indicated by the time-signature for each instance of analysis. The subjective utility is individual and formed after the objective utility is determined. Two decision makers, for example, confronted with a closed information system, may choose to act on the system and contribute to the dynamics the system generates; or they may choose to reject it, perhaps making their decisions in favor of another system. For decision making, the element of uncertainty is greater in the open system than in the closed, for the closed system is static while the open system is fluid, with fluctuating and contradictory information being added, in spite of its closure by the time-signature of each decision maker in his deliberations. Yet the decision maker treats both systems as closed and studies their probabilities to assess their objective utilities; and when his own subjective utility is accounted for, the decision maker makes his choice with regard to the consequences he desires.

In this sense, subjective utility reflects the projected results, that is, the future consequences desired by the decision maker. It is based on weighing the present against the future, whose degrees of uncertainty are related directly to the extent determined by the objective utility. Subjective utility is derived from the decision maker's personal ordering of preferences, which he bases on the consequences he desires from the system, as these are weighed with respect to alternative systems, with the uncertainty of the future an important consideration.

The ordering of preferences requires, therefore, that each alternative information system under consideration be ranked, first with regard to its objective utility and then in terms of its personal subjective utility. Thus, there is a relationship between the subjective utility as determined by the decision maker and the objective utility determined by the system's probability assessments. Should the decision maker act in favor of a system, this relationship is positive; should he act against the system, the relationship is negative. Economic activity is generated by the quantity of positive relationships among decision makers and information systems, for by utilizing these information systems, decision makers institute programs, money is invested, and purchases are made. Those information systems that are inactive soon succumb to entropy.

The positive or negative relationship depends on the decision maker's objectives and the system's content. Should the decision maker have a preset goal and all available information systems fail to provide sufficient inducement for the satisfaction of this goal, then the decision maker will remain inactive. This, however, is an extreme case and more likely the decision maker would have established modified goals in case his best goal situation proves unrealistic with regard to the information systems available. He will then act on that system that provides him the best future situation as determined by the modified goal, with this new goal becoming the best case.

Schematically, this objective-subjective relationship can be stated thus: $Eu\mathrm{A} = F(P, \mathrm{A})$, meaning that expected or subjective utility of information system A is a function of A with regard to its objective probability content. With A's objective utility approaching the maximum limit, there is no necessary bearing on Eu/A, on the expected utility of A, for this is strictly subjective and objective A may yield consequences unwanted or considered irrelevant by the decision maker. Hence, for one decision maker concerned with a specific problem area $[Eu\mathrm{A}/ = F(P, \mathrm{A})]_{t_1} \rightarrow 1$, while for another decision maker concerned with approximately the same area $Eu/\mathrm{A}_{t_1} \rightarrow 0$. Nor are these subjective assessments permanent over time, for they are often altered with the acquisition of greater understanding and/or the changing ordering of preferences; thus, while A may have been rejected because of low subjective utility in t_1, in a different time period t_n $(n > 1)$, the subjective reordering and possible shifts in A's information content in the case of an open system may result in A receiving a very high subjective ordering position.

Because decision makers consider systems and make decisions on the basis of objective and subjective utilities, the sum total of these actions is the sum total of economic activity. Although utility is a sufficient explanation for decision-making activity, it does not explain why decisions are not made with respect to alternative information systems. Moreover, the difficulties of the open information system over time result in a reduction of utility, with information systems being eventually reduced by the impact that decision making has on them for other decision makers. Acting upon a system brings about a change in the information content. Investing in shares when their market prices are low, for example, drives up the prices. Or, entering a highly competitive imitative market reduces the profits of the other imitative firms. This reduction of utility is entropy.[3]

Entropy in its objective sense, is the measurement of disinformation in an information system. It illustrates the extent to which the system's elements, that is statements, do *not* relate to their objective realities, thereby providing a basis for discrimination and choice, which are subjective. Symbolized by the letter H, the entropy of an information system A indicates the extent to which some or all of A's statements no longer correspond to the realities for which they were designed and intended. Just as utility is measured between the lower and upper boundaries, so is entropy, and thus it is the negation of utility. Where the utility of $\mathrm{A} \rightarrow 1$, the entropy of $\mathrm{A} \rightarrow 0$, and *vice versa*.

Since the closed information system designates a reality that is relevant only for the period stated by its time-signature, the only way this system can be threatened with entropy is if it is revised and its reality altered. Take, for example, the system that states facts 1,2, •••, n, bounded by a certain date in the future. If one or more of its statements are altered to correspond to change for the period of time stated, this system can become entropic. If one of its factual statements is altered because of a change in the reality it describes, the entire system is brought into a declining objective utility rating. However, the rating can be raised by a reformulation of the statement in light of the changing reality. This is a technical adjustment, for the system has become objectively entropic because the shift in reality makes it irrelevant.

Of course, it is possible that such a shift in reality could become so extreme that the information system per se would no longer have any utility and would therefore have to be abandoned completely. In the case of the merger of two firms, cited earlier, should one of the managers suddenly pass away and thus bring instability to the firm, the merger and plans for joint production would likely be terminated, at least until the time when the managerial board could establish an acceptable replacement and reinstate the merger plans to the satisfaction of the other firm. There is no time-signature placed here, and the objective entropy has replaced utility, thus breaking down the information system entirely.

For the open information system, objective analysis must account for the utility of A being dependent on the probability of its statements relating to reality, so that the information I of A equals the probability of A being relevant, that is, $I/A_{t_1} = P/A_{t_1}$, with A at time t_1 containing a closed number of statements as determined by the time-signature. If the probability assessment indicates that absolutely no relationship exists between the statements and their prescribed realities, then $I = H$ and the entire system is devoid of utility. Of course, should the probabilities correspond totally during the period of time, then $I \equiv -H$ and the system enjoys full objective utility.

This either-or situation in which either entropy or utility prevails in its extreme is the best of all possible worlds and is thus difficult, if not impossible, to achieve. Information systems are formulated to correspond to their specific realities; it is unlikely that they will be either totally irrelevant or absolutely perfect, perfection not being a human trait, especially in the realm of economic activity. More likely the situation is that some degree of entropy exists in the open-ended system because of a slight shift in the reality even though the system is studied with the time-signature acting as a restriction, or perhaps an inadequate relationship was formulated for a statement or statements within the system that do not adequately define their realities.

In short, just as absolute utility is almost impossible to achieve for a bounded system, absolute entropy is equally as difficult. It is only when a sufficiently large proportion of the system's statements show an absence of relevance to their realities that the system should be considered sufficiently objectively entropic to be abandoned and other alternative systems should be sought.

Objective determination of the level of entropy for an open information system is achieved by assessing the probabilities of the system's statements with respect to the reality for which these statements are constructed. For example, the system A_{t_1} has utility approaching the maximum limit—were this not the case, the system would not be stated as it is—and over the period between time 1 and time 2, changes occur in either the reality or the content of A, or perhaps both. The assessment of A's utility and entropy requires the evaulation of the statements. These statements may contain glaring inadequacies that can be either corrected forthright or cast out of the system; it is likely that these inadequacies are due to the incorporation of statements that have a better definitive relationship to their realities. These provide little difficulty and once removed or corrected strengthen A's utility.

The difficulties arise with those statements whose subtle discrepancies affect seriously the utility of A yet are not subject to alteration because any alteration would result in A's being drastically changed, perhaps to the point of bringing the entire information system to a state of extreme entropy and hence dissolution. This is due to the cumulative influence of the shifting statements and/or changing realities, rendering A as such of little utility. A firm may set out to undertake a production project and thus establish its information system in order to attract investors and encourage consumption of its product. There may be discrepancies between the production plans and the actual production processes, due to either human inadequacy or mechanical failures. The consequence is that production targets are not quite met and the planned economies of production not realized. These discrepancies are not noticed until the feedback from production and consumption is analyzed. The consequence is that the A_t system moves toward an entropic condition as its utility declines. Such a movement toward entropy is not serious if caught in time and A can be revised to cope with the more realistic conditions prevailing in the production processes and the markets. The information statements can be revised and the entropy temporarly removed, so that $A_t \neq A_{t_1}$, and that $A_{t_1} \nrightarrow 1$.

The dynamics of production and marketing are such, however, that new discrepancies arise that are not accounted for in A_{t_1}, so that over time, this too will become entropic. The reconstruction process is continued to the point that the entropy that finally evolves renders the entire A system of little utility and economically not worth the effort to reconstruct further. Increased competition, for example, may lower the firm's profit-cost ratio to the extent that any "new" changes in the product's composition would not offset the costs involved. Market saturation may then be so extensive that the product line can be maintained only at a loss, either with respect to continuing the production or with consideration for the greater profit potential to be gained from alternative projects. The decision maker must then choose to maintain the product at its current profit-cost ratio, keeping the advertising level sufficient to hold sales in light of the strenuous competition, or to close down production and allocate resources otherwise. Should the product be maintained, then A is acted upon by management to remain stable within its utility boundaries; should the decision be taken to abandon the product, then entropy is immediately introduced and the system is rendered completely entropic and beyond reconstruction. The latter decision is final while the former still preserves the dynamics of the product, which will remain active until a decision taken in the future phases it out, or until the economy changes because of its general dynamics and consumer demand no longer supports the product but is allocated in other directions.

Discrepancies exist also as a direct result of the information system. Revised production plans, no matter how slight, result in the development of other difficulties not considered by the system. Differing production techniques instituted to gain economics of costs will incur difficulties not considered in the revised information system, such as bottlenecks in moving the product in the markets. Improved production techniques, for example, yield greater output at either lower aggregate costs or lower production yields at the same costs. In the first instance, the market may not be able to absorb the increased output, and so sales prices have to be reduced to make the product more appealing to a consumer population already confronted with competitive close substitutes. Reduced sales prices mean reduced profits, so that greater output due to increased production efficiency may not yield higher profits in the medium and long runs. In the second instance, lower production yields result from a planned inefficient use of the techniques, so that while full capacity is not being used, it cannot be redirected to other projects; the result is a net loss. Output capacity is thus restricted—a situation that close competitors will not necessarily respect; indeed, they will tend to saturate the market as completely as their own internal and external economies will allow, at the expense of the firm's production restraint.

In short, an open-ended information system is subject to entropy at all times. Even though its information content is fixed by its time-signature when presented, the realities of the situation result in changing de facto probability measurements between the system's statements and the realities to which these statements relate. The time-signature indicates the system's objective entropy and utility ratings for the period signified; but as time changes, so do these ratings, not as a function of time, but as a consequence of the events that occur. Only through analysis can the extent of these changes be understood and their causes determined. The ratings of information systems are undertaken periodically, especially when there is reason to suspect possible disinformation. Nevertheless, their objective positions are changing as a result of alterations in their defined realities, which can be detected only by proper assessment.

Unlike the case with objective entropy, subjective entropy is not necessarily reflexive. An information system may be approaching maximum objective utility yet be considered entropic by an individual who has a different preference of ordering for the area defined by the information system, in which case he may choose to support an alternative system that has a lower utility rating but is not sufficiently entropic to be troublesome. It is unlikely, however, that a rational individual will opt for a system with a low utility rating rather than support one whose rating is high. The individual may prefer not to act at all, to wait and see what happens over a time span he determines to be significant, in which he behaves as if all systems are entropic even though their objective ratings indicate otherwise. This latter case is rational and personal; it depends on the individual's liquidity and his understanding of the possibilities in the time he assigns for his waiting and acting.

Subjective entropy is therefore due to personal assessment that depends on the ordering of preferences with respect to the psychological aspect of expectation. Since expectation is related to reality by the understanding of current events and how these events may influence the future, preferences for choosing to work with an information system or opting not to are reality based, to the best understanding of the individual. Hence, while $A_{o_t} \rightarrow 1$ (the subscript *o* meaning objective) $A_{s_t} \rightarrow 0$ (*s* meaning subjective). However, $A_{s_{t_n}}$ may have a very high subjective utility rating, with t_n being a time in the assigned future, beyond the present time-signature.

Unlike objective entropy and utility, subjective entropy and utility cannot be analyzed with respect to probabilities of the various information statements as they relate to their respective areas. Entropy, in its subjective form, may be due to personal whims, improper or incomplete understanding of the information, or a waiting for alternatives that are expected to be more viable but that may not materialize when the future is finally reached. Although there is no real accounting for individual tastes and preferences, economic activity seeks to control these individual properties, focusing them on consumer products, investment opportunities, and production projects.

Just as with subjective utility and its impact on objective utility, subjective entropy has an impact on the directions economic activity takes. The decision to operate within one information system is taken at the expense of other possible systems. Since working within a system influences the system's statements, altering their relationships to their realities, rejecting a system because of subjective entropy will affect the system in a negative manner. For the closed system such a rejection inhibits its dynamics from being realized, to the extent of the impact brought about by the concerned populace's rejection. For the closed information system defines a specific set of circumstances that are valid for the period indicated by the time-signature. This system is formulated and stated for people concerned with the area to act on. It is to bring investors into the arrangement, to initiate production, to sell products. Should this system be ignored, that is, should the population to which it is directed not respond due to subjective entropy, then its objective utility will decline rapidly and entropy will be so intensive that the system will dissolve. This is the extreme case, but the extent of objective entropy as far as the system's relevance to its populace is concerned will be determined by the degree of response by those willing to opt for the system. A system without takers, no matter how efficient it is internally, will collapse.

The situation for the open system is different. The system is formulated to relate to an area that cannot be closed by the system's statements. Dynamics within the area require the statements to be revised or discarded as need be. Also, new statements have to be formulated; these are of utility as long as they conform to the general probability rating of the system and thereby maintain the overall utility. The dynamics of the system, in this sense, depend on the populace that works with it. Take, for example, the extreme case of an open-ended information system without anyone to work it. It will soon collapse because of the objective entropy generated by the changing area for which it was formulated. Subjective entropy, the preference ordering that keeps the populace away from the system, will thus bring about objective entropy and the system's dissolution. The extreme case is unlikely here too, for the extent of objective entropy, in this sense, depends on the degree with which people choose to avoid the system.

The qualifier "in this sense" is important, for it indicates one way that subjective entropy influences objective entropy. In the closed information system, subjective entropy influences objective entropy in another way. It acts on the system before the time-signature is realized, thereby disrupting its objective utility. For example, a system states that at a certain date, conditions x, y, and z will occur. A disagreement ensues over the accepted system's terminology and statements. One individual decides to take action to render the system entropic before anyone else can realize what is happening. Thus, due to subjective entropy—that is, his rejection of the system despite the good intentions of others to carry it out—the individual acts to prevent one of the conditions—say y—from being fulfilled. Since the closed system is so constructed that all statements have to hold together and relate to their realities exactly as expressed, altering one of the statements, statement y, will bring down the entire system. Subjective entropy thus inspires action that generates objective entropy and a collapse of the program, deal, or whatever the situation may be.

For the open system, the situation is different. In this system—and here we must assume that it is at maximum utility, so that no objective entropy has yet occurred—a person may disagree with a specific relationship between a statement and its reality; he may change the statement, bringing it farther away from the probability that existed previously. Enough dynamics will be generated to require the statements to change. Should this process continue to any length and extent, however, then the system will be brought to an entropic condition before its "natural decline," which would have come about by the changing realities and the inability to alter the statements according to them. Personal subjective entropy may thus tamper with a system of high utility; the extent and duration of this activity based on subjective entropy determines the swiftness of the system's demise over its natural course.

In the world of economic activity, nevertheless, the drive for profits and the search for alternative production projects tend to keep the participants in the economic arena rational, with *rational* understood to mean relating to economic events and acting on them according to their own best interests. This definition seeks to exclude *irrational*, that is, noneconomic, behavior to minimize activities that disturb competition and the search for profits. Thus, investing in shares without considering portfolios or spreading the liquidity to hedge against uncertainty, establishing a production line for a project not yet researched, or making economic decisions without recognizing the possible consequences are excluded in this definition, as they are minimal and have little impact on economic activity.

It is therefore the case that contrary to the fears and suspicions of a great many people the world over, inflation and unemployment are manageable, their socioeconomic consequences need not be overbearing, and viable decision-making in government and business circles can be undertaken according to the state of current disequilibrium.

Rational decision makers of course have their preferences and their subjective utilities and entropies influence and are influenced by their understandings of their information systems and the realities being defined. The economist must deal with decision making, be it based on subjective, objective, or combined considerations–this latter case being the most likely. The profit motive is the driving force in decision making, for without gain there would be no undertaking. The extent of profit taking and the sacrifices of profit ratios to costs have been termed maximizing and satisficing; these must now be discussed and their roles in economics explained.

ON MAXIMIZING AND SATISFICING

It is important to note that the term *profit*, traditionally used in the business sector to mean revenue that remains after costs are deducted, has another meaning in this discussion. It is used here to mean the achievement of objectives after the alternative costs and business operating expenses have been deducted. Hence, when used in discussing profits in decision making, the term refers to business profits and government profits, where alternative costs of other projects are discounted as relevant and after-accounting costs, that is, business costs for the entire economy, are considered. The profit motive, as used here, contrasts with the concepts of maximizing.

According to neoclassical economic theory, the ideal situation for a firm is when its profits are maximized with its costs maintained at a low, economically efficient level. Neoclassical theory treats the firm as sufficiently small with its manager, the entrepreneur, alert for new market trends and new projects. As the "economic man," the neoclassical manager is motivated strictly by those projects that yield the highest profits, with the profit motive bringing him into as many diversified areas as his business can support.

The investor in neoclassical theory seeks to place his liquidity in those projects that offer the highest yield for the lowest risk. Hence, the profit motive here is the only driving force, and so the investor, also an "economic man," searches for projects that will provide the highest profit-risk ratio, with alternative projects being rejected because either the profits are too low or the risks too high. Speculation in neoclassical theory is offset by hedging against alternative projects. The "economic investor" will not place all his liquidity in one project but distribute it according to the profit-risk ratios of the various investment opportunities.

Since the advent of managerial capitalism, however, some economists claim that the profit motive has lost its position as the prime mover of economic activity. The complexities of contemporary markets, coupled with the intense competition, have reduced the "lion's share" approach to entrepreneurial activity to that of satisficing. This has been further enhanced by the swift retooling activities of close competitors due to increasingly sophisticated technologies. Accurate market projections reduce the element of risk when close imitative substitutes are projected for innovative markets, with entrepreneurial innovation an extremely short run affair, with profits registered accordingly. The status of profit maximization, so revered in neoclassical theory, has thus fallen, to be replaced by satisficing.

Satisficing, according to Marris, is the behavior

> in which the subject, faced with a difficult problem to solve, prefers to sacrifice some of the rewards of the optimum solution in order to reduce the pains incurred in searching for it. Rather than maximize, he chooses to "satisfice," i.e., to accept some solution which is "good enough" in relation to various criteria such as survival, aspiration or avoidance of pain.[4]

That this psychological concept has become a part of managerial economics is shown in an article by Professor H. A. Simon, one of the pioneers of satisficing in economics. Professor Simon wrote that models of satisficing behavior are richer than models of maximizing behavior because they deal not only with equilibrium but also with methods of reaching equilibrium. In these models of satisficing the decision-maker's aspiration level defines a natural zero-point on the utility scale, compared with the neoclassical approach in which, according to Professor Simon, the aspiration level is arbitrary. Because the decision maker in neoclassical theory is identified with the entrepreneur, his aspiration level is that of his firm's, so that the entrepreneur's maximum aspiration level limits his firm's goals to those projects that yield only the maximum utility. Opting for the satisficing position can, however, allow the entrepreneur to develop strategies that allow the firm optimum positions instead of seeking only the maximum, which are unattainable. Hence, the difference between neoclassical and managerial economics. Neoclassical theory stresses only profit maximization, while the proponents of managerial economics argue that the conditions are such that maximization is unattainable and must be replaced by optimal conditions. According to Professor Simon,

> When the firm has alternatives open to it that are at or above its aspiration level, the theory predicts that it will choose the best of those known to be available. When none of the available alternatives satisfies current aspirations, the theory predicts qualitatively different behavior: in the short run, search behavior and the revision of targets; in the longer run, what we have called above emotional behavior and what the psychologist would be inclined to call neurosis.[5]

Psychoses and neuroses aside, Marris describes one way in which a firm satisfices; this is when a firm maintains a sustainable but nonoptimal growth rate by deliberately setting an above-optimum retention ratio, thereby providing the maximum sustainable growth rate at its satisficing level, that is, by setting the growth rate at a level lower than that which can be achieved and thus increasing the ratio of the firm's market value to net assets and operating with this value (ν) constrained. This ratio can be passed on in the future in the form of higher prices demanded for new share issues, allowing for the increase in the gearing ratio of liabilities to assets[6] and according to the market demand for these shares.

According to Professor Simon, the satisficing models are the only models valid for describing the contemporary firm's operations. Such practices as those mentioned by Marris are legitimate and indeed operable in corporate decision making. Moreover, the theory of the managerial firm is important in welfare economics to determine under what circumstances the firm's behavior will lead to an efficient allocation of resources. From this, Professor Simon comments that

> the satisficing model vitiates all the conclusions about resource allocation and are derivable from the maximizing model when perfect competition is assumed. Similarly, a dynamic theory of firm sizes, . . . has quite different implications for public policies dealing with concentration than a theory that assumes firms to be in static equilibrium.[7]

In this comment Professor Simon identified the problem with satisficing—that it is effective only when dynamic equilibrium prevails, for in such a setting firms of different sizes compete and equilibrium is maintained in spite of each firm's ability to control its resource potential and its share of the market. By maintaining that welfare economics is a static branch of the discipline, he implies that the allocation of resources for welfare recipients is affected by those conditions in the equilibrium economy that bring about change. According to this dynamic framework, the necessity for resource allocation exists and is controlled by the dynamic state essential for maintaining growth and stability, underwritten by governmental monetary and fiscal policies.

Yet, the question here is not one of dynamics or statics for those firms whose policies have necessary implications for the distribution of national wealth, the composition and level of aggregate employment, and the structure and distribution of productive liquidity and capital. In post-World War II the use of statics has been merely for analysis and neither for micro nor macro policy formulation. The de facto dynamics have been those not of equilibrium but of disequilibrium, with welfare considerations changing accordingly. The difficulty with the satisficing approach to contemporary decision making is accepting that since the advent of managerial economics the area of concern is the generation of market dynamics for new products, the maintaining of those products that retain an accepted profit-cost ratio, and the phasing out of those products whose profit-cost ratio is unacceptable. The derivation of satisficing conditions from maximizing models where perfect competition is assumed is, again, a technique for analysis—important perhaps for the formulation of policy alternatives, but no more than that. Releasing the perfect-competition restraint brings the model closer to reality; it also allows for greater flexibility between maximizing and satisficing. The point is, however, that the closer the model approaches the realistic condition, the closer maximizing and satisficing become.

This can be seen in Marris's example. His firm maintains a sustainable but nonoptimum growth rate, achieved by raising the optimal retention ratio, with the consequence of reducing the potentially maximum sustainable growth rate. The purpose of lowering the growth rate is to exert influence on the gearing ratio, thereby increasing liquidity. This is a trade-off between liquidity and growth; because no economic actions are taken without external and internal reasons, the logic of this trade-off is apparent. A sluggish market and declining sales, for example, result in a growth rate lower than in optimum conditions. Lower sales mean lower profits, which reduce capital liquidity available for financing other prospective projects. A higher retention ratio than otherwise available when left strictly to market forces allows for the release of greater resources and hence provides for more flexibility in programming and producing. By raising the optimum retention ratio the firm is thus in a more viable competitive position allowing for the shifting of production priorities according to market conditions; it is thereby better poised for generating new markets where product and consumer response warrant.

By raising the optimum retention ratio the firm has greater utility, increasing its viability with respect to other competing firms. With this increased utility comes an increase in the firm's maximizing position. Thus, the reasons stated earlier provide ample evidence that should the retention ratio remain fixed in terms of present, that is, static, market conditions, the firm will be in a position of dynamic equilibrium, shifting its policies as its markets change. The firm will not, however, be in control to the extent of setting its own policies independent of the market because of its isomorphic dependence on its markets.

This shows that it is incorrect to argue that by increasing the retention ratio, satisficing is obtained. What is achieved is a maximal position of the firm as a dynamic force in the economy, with the retention ratio raised to the level that allows the greatest flexibility for the firm and hence the maximum level of achievable profits, restrained only by the market conditions and responses to the firm's policies. Raising the retention ratio prevents the firm's decision-making processes from becoming entirely dependent on the market's whims, allowing policies to be set that will allow consumers to try the firm's products and divert their liquidity ratios according to their individual preferences. Satisficing becomes maximizing and is undertaken to ensure that the firm achieves maximum profits. If strict satisficing were the case, the firm would be entirely at the market's mercy, lacking the ability to exert an independent influence. However, the dynamic firm in nonequilibrium brings new products into the market, stabilizing those products that show an acceptable profit level and phasing out those products whose profit levels are unacceptable. This nonequilibrium and dynamic situation demonstrates that satisficing is in fact maximizing, for the firm establishes policies that will obtain the highest profit levels given the constraints placed on the firm.

The case with investments is similar. In a dynamic disequilibrium market, hedging and investing in short- and long-term projects depend most certainly on the expected utilities of these projects. An educated investor will diversify his portfolio according to the proposals at his disposal and the conditions of the market. Instead of receiving maximum yields on one investment by placing his liquidity entirely in that project—and risk losses that may occur because of a fickle market—the investor will spread his money, thereby ensuring the highest aggregate returns and having the greatest maneuverability to cope with market changes. Where maximizing calls for seeking the highest profits, the wise investor avoids seeking such profits in a single investment project. Instead, satisficing is the strategy he uses, seeking acceptable profits from each project that, when taken in the aggregate, provide the highest maximum profit rate. Moreover, the ability to maneuver ensures the freedom to maintain this profit level in light of changes affecting the investments.

It is only because of utility that satisficing is equated with maximizing in operative behavior. For in rational economic behavior—*rational* meaning being motivated by economic realities only—it is economic utility which is sought. In the example of investments, placing total liquidity in a single portfolio to achieve the portfolio's highest return on investment subjects both the investor and the investment to the whims of the market, leaving the investor without room for maneuvering, subjecting his money to a decline in value and disutility and thus rendering his investment entropic.

The case with managerial decision making is also similar: Utility equates maximizing and satisficing, as in the earlier example with the retention ratio. By setting the retention ratio to the level that provides the greatest flexibility and hence the maximum achievable profits, the decision maker can obtain sufficient maneuverability to formulate and act upon projects that would not have been undertaken had the retention ratio remained unaltered. This is a manifestation of utility, for by altering the retention ratio, decision making is provided with greater scope and the firm's performance in competition is enhanced. Indeed, the main reason for initiating such a policy is to overcome entropic conditions that exist as either potential threats or real factors confronting the firm and reducing its viability as a profit-making organization.

The firm's and the investor's economic positions depend on specific decision-making processes and the economy's responses to these dynamics. Utility and entropy are both responses to and determining factors of the firm and investor and most certainly the economy, which in turn responds and places constraints on the decision makers' maneuverabilities. Government officials concerned with economics are also subject to maximized satisficing, as the constraints with which they seek to maneuver can respond only along the patterns established by the general macroeconomic movement. This will be treated later, but it suffices now to state that the government and businesspeople, acting out of different interests and from different perspectives, must share the common position that a healthy economy is one that is in dynamic disequilibrium; they must operate according to this view, from their individual points, to prevent a breaking down of the managerial economic system and a looming prolonged and intense world depression.

ON THE THEORY OF VALUE

A favorite theme in the works of economics is seeking to determine the causes of value, the reasons why people labor to purchase certain items, and to seek the mysterious manner in which value is imputed to an object or event. A difficulty in determining economic value is that economists claim that their discipline is a science, with analytic, descriptive, and predictive powers normally attributed to the physical sciences. Analytic ability is, however, not restricted to the physical sciences and therefore economists can have claim to that power; with the advent of quantum physics and relativity theory, the descriptive and predictive powers of physics are certainly questionable.

What should not be questioned is that if economics is to obtain a respectability of its own, its practitioners must not seek to rely on the already-achieved prestige of other disciplines but seek to strengthen their own. It is no longer viable to impute value, say, to the work force, to the consequences of bartering, and most definitely not to the all-encompassing phrases of supply and demand. Nor should value, so important a part in the development of economics, be cast aside as an adolescent growing pain. For the significance of value is that it provides the basis for each transaction, the decision for or against each productive project, and the basis for government interaction in the economy.

If this is so, then why has a theory of value been so difficult to establish? Why, for example, has not Marx's labor theory of value resulted in the downfall of the managerial capitalistic system? Why have the communist countries been confronted with the problems of production and employment Marx claimed would vanish in the communist state?

Marx's interpretation and those of the other economists have been irrelevant for a simple reason—one fundamental to scientific inquiry. They approached the theory of value from a position of bias without seeking to understand if their theories are realistic and have roles to play in economics.

A theory in science must be both relevant and workable, not in the future, but now. Marx's predictions have failed because he based his theory of value on unrealistic assumptions. Supply and demand cannot prove to be theories of value because of their vagueness, which leaves room for many interpretations. The bartering process in the market place cannot offer a satisfactory value theory because although a selling price is agreed on, the question is unanswered why the barter was undertaken in the first place—and this, a theory of value must answer.

The concepts of utility and entropy in their expression of satisficing-maximizing form a theory of value that meets the scientific requirement of being derived from reality and being used to explain it. Utility is both subjective and objective; in its subjective state, it affects the economy only when the individual acts. Objective utility is thus influenced through the action. The same is the case with entropy: It is manifested subjectively through choosing alternatives, but its objective manifestations are noted through the decline of force previously held.

Economics as a science must focus on people as "economic" beings, acting rationally to their best advantage. Hence, people impute value according to their understanding of utility and entropy, which is why there is no necessity for two "economic" individuals to have the same value schedule, since their interpretations of utility and entropy for the same projects may differ. Acting to maximize under the restrictive satisficing conditions, individuals choose their purchases and make their decisions according to their personal utility-entropy scales. Because these are related to the economy in the aggregate, they provide a picture of total value, which may, in turn, influence consumers in the manner Marris explained with his treatment of sheeplike behavior. It is in the aggregate that value becomes objective and is manifested in forms of commerce and decision making.

Hence, the requirement of deriving a theory from reality and applying it to its reality is accomplished. Indeed, objective value is nothing more than the total of the utility and entropy schedules as maximizing is undertaken by all economic people subject to the satisficing constraints. This, then, is the impact that these total utility and entropy schedules have on the economy as people seek the maximum, constrained by satisficing.

THE INFORMATION SYSTEM AND ITS ALTERATIONS

The closed and open information systems are considered here with respect to their required alterations because of the impact of entropy. The purpose of these alterations is to preserve the systems' integrity until they are abandoned totally when they no longer have utility or until they can be replaced by other systems.

For both systems, the elements of the system describe and delineate the realities to which they refer. These elements are therefore the information statements about the realities for which they are constructed and as such also tell what the realities do not contain. These information statements, or elements, are isomorphic, with each element referring to only one aspect of reality confined in the information system, the scope of which is contained within the terms of the element. These elements are also reflexive in the sense that as each element relates only to its specific particle of reality, that particle of reality relates only to its unique element. When first established, these relationships lack the difficulties of ambiguity, of meta languages and meta information systems.

The system A therefore contains the information elements and the reality for which these elements are constructed. Stated another way, A if and only if R, with R being the defined reality. Hence, $A = [A, R]$, with the elements in A corresponding isomorphically and reflexively to the particles in R.

In the closed information system entropy sets in only when the reality alters and the elements no longer retain their isomorphism, with the reflexivity destroyed. For example, a firm floats a bond to finance a specific product that is defined and for which the specific consumer classes are delineated. The production procedure is explained, with all the costing and intended profit ratios expressed. This occurs in time t_1. The difficulty is that no matter how much control over a market situation the firm exerts, the factor of uncertainty may be reduced but never eliminated. In t_2, for instance, a minor economic crisis in a different sector may affect the aggregate interest rates on loans, making this particular project unprofitable as an investment or even as an undertaking for the firm. In view of this, should the project be continued, the information presented must relate to the new reality, as a result of extraneous circumstances the firm cannot control. What the source of this change in the information content is makes no difference; what is important is to note how the change is made.

Given R' as the new reality, system A must also be altered. Consider the relationship $a_d r$; that is, information element a defines the reality r. When r alters to become r', its defining element must also change to become a' in order to maintain its defining relationship. The shift from r to r' renders a inadequate, and so the relationship has become entropic. Entropy can be reversed by combining with a relevant bits of information that cover the change in r without destroying the general import of the defining element. Hence, with a altered to a', yet with the import of the original defining element still intact, r' is covered and the relationship remains viable.

What has been considered here is a slight shift in R, with but a very few elements affected. Should a majority of elements be affected by a radical change in the reality, either A will be abandoned, with the entire information system becoming completely entropic and discarded, or a new definitive relationship between A and R will be constructed, maintaining those parts that have retained their viability while building relationships from the changed reality. However, should such a reconstruction be deemed unprofitable because of the uncertainty, then further market research, not worth the cost involved, will be abandoned and no attempt at reconstruction will be undertaken.

What is unique to the open system is that its elements and its reality are both subject to alterations. Because of the openness, the likelihood for entropy at any given moment is greater for the open system than for the closed system. When entropy does attack the open system, however, it is usually not as devastating as it is with the closed system. The open system thus has a greater ability to salvage itself than has the closed system.

Whereas in the closed system entropy results from changes only in its reality, which must be met with changes in the definitive and delineating elements, changes in the open system can come from either side of the relationship, that is, from changes in its reality or from changes in its elements. This leads to greater definitive power and sharper distinctions within the system, but it also tends to blur the isomorphism because of a precision that may cut too fine.

Three reasons for entropy in the open system must be considered. First, there may be a change in the reality of the situation defined by the elements. For example, system A contains the elements of A and R, so that $R \sum \mathrm{A}/\mathrm{A}_d R_t$. As both A and R are open ended, the definitive relationship holds for those elements restricted by the time-signature. At time t, n relationships exist; in t_1, the eth particle in n is altered due to a shift in the reality of this particle, which alters e but not to the extent that e's identity is totally destroyed. Because of this alteration, the defining element must also be altered; but as this system is open ended, care must be taken not to interfere with the other relationships. This situation is similar to, but not identical with, the change that occurs in the closed system. The difference here is one of nuance; yet it is significant because changes in the reality in the particle in question can come about from changes in other relationships. The repairing process may therefore affect the other relationships, either directly or indirectly. This change may be due to the improvement of information in the reality that renders the entire relationship entropic and thus ineffective; it may be due to a deterioration in a particular aspect of reality that calls for a better definitive element. It may also be due to the merging of two or more reality particles due to information that eliminates the nuances that bring about the necessity for separate elements for definition and demarcation. The specific instances of change must be met with appropriate alterations in the definitive elements and in their corresponding realities if the information system's viability is to be maintained and entropy eliminated.

An example of this situation is a country that has a loan scheme initiated by the central banking system and provided by the major banking organizations. The loan's terms are well defined and the interest rate stated. The isomorphic and reflexive definitive-reality statements are clearly delineated, yet further government policy—and not that of the banking organizations—bear directly on the de facto interest rate and the terms of the scheme. Where the scheme is subject to alteration, changing conditions in the markets can allow for coping with these alterations, either within the terms of the original scheme or in the guise of other schemes that maintain the fixed terms and conditions while allowing for the variability of the reality requiring the redefinition of those elements affected by these changes.

The second reason for entropy in the open information system is the improvement in the quality of defining information and the manner in which this improvement brings about a break in the isomorphic and reflexive relationships. The consequence is that the statement $a_d r$

if $r_d a$, meaning that *a* defines *r* if and only if *r* is defined by *a*, so that changes in the defining element, no matter how small, must be met by changes in that reality particle if the isomorphic-reflexive relationship is to be maintained. Due to the greater understanding of the problem over time allowed by the time-signature, *a* may change; nevertheless, the reality particle remains static while the defining language, being sharpened, opens new vistas for dealing with reality. When proposals for new markets were considered, market nuances may not have been thoroughly explored. Thus, as the new product enters the market, further understanding of the market requires redefinition of the product's capabilities and the consumer class for which the product was originally intended. Differences in the nuances in product projection as publicized through advertising cover these fields, leaving the reality, which in this case is the market, to adjust.

The third reason for entropy in the open information system is that changes take place in the defining elements, due to a refinement of information, *and* in the realities, independent of and not corresponding to changes in the defining elements. In this situation appropriate adjustments must be made on both sides of the definition if the relationship, and ultimately the system, is to be maintained. An innovative product captures its intended market, for example, and thereby defines it. Claims made for the product are substantiated by its consumption rate and the profit rate. A successful product is defined as that which brings about a reallocation of consumer liquidity as measured by the per capita income liquidity devoted to the product. Such a product brings into its market close substitutes, thereby altering the initial reality of the product's unique success. A refinement in information through advertising seeks to siphon sales from the competitors, while the reality over time might not correspond to the situation desired by the managers. The reality might indicate a drastic and dangerous decline in sales, indicating the ineffectiveness of the new advertising campaign. The reality is thus to be adjusted by various managerial tactics such as satisficing-maximizing and seeking to maintain the product's commercial viability through sales promotions. Should these prove successful in light of the rigorous competition, then the information system and the firm's profits are maintained until further changes are indicated; should these fail, it is likely that managerial decision making will phase out the product and channel the released productive resources into other innovative and imitative production.

In both the closed and the open information system entropy sets in most often when these systems are not able to handle changes in the reality through reconstructing their terms and statements. The long-run consequence of entropy is either diversification while maintaining the product as best as possible or abandonment of the project, directing the released resources elsewhere. The automobile industry, for example, has altered radically the concept of motorized transportation and the energy crisis has led to new techniques for fuel economy and utility. Another example is a well-known soft drink that has not been altered since its first marketing, while its presentation and advertising campaign have most certainly been kept up with the trends and times. Diversification in the automobile industry has not only resulted in manifold modes of transportation to suit varied requirements and tastes; it has also led to better roads and stricter competition from other forms of transportation. This one soft drink has maintained its unique identity while being introduced in many countries and stimulating competition.

The point is that for every information system A, given a change in either a or in r—and in the case of the open system only, given changes in both—viability is maintained as long as alterations are made in the changed elements and the system's utility is kept intact as a total information system. Should the appropriate changes not be made, the system begins to become entropic at an increasing rate, bringing about the system's decline. Economic activity requires that such alterations be made when necessary; otherwise, the necessity of profit maximization—in private business activity and government economic decision making—will establish the conditions by which the projects in question will be abandoned and replaced.

PROBLEMS OF MARGINALISM AND THE APPLICATION OF UTILITY

The concept of Marginalism has been extremely important in the development of economic theory, yet it is not without its difficulties. Two applications of Marginalism are discussed here and their difficulties analyzed and then resolved by the application of utility.

Marginalism teaches that the most efficient use of a firm's resources in production is reached when the receipts gained from producing one more product are equal to the added production costs involved in manufacturing that single product, that is, when marginal cost equals marginal revenue. It is at this level that the productive resources engaged in the product's manufacture are at their maximum efficiency; if production occurs below this level, facilities are still available for increasing production, and if all production occurs above this level, it is either prevented by the limitations of the firm's resources or restricted by losses sustained because revenues from increased production are less than production costs.

Marginal cost can be stated thus: $MC = p - VC$, where p is the price and VC is the variable cost of production. VC is the cost of improving the seller's offer sufficiently by raising the sale by one or more production units; alternatively, the VC is the savings gained by offering the market less attractive terms, leading to the decline in sales of one or more units. For every sale there must be a buyer; thus, the elasticity of demand is expressed by $e = p/VC$, which can be rewritten as $e = p \, \Delta \, q/q \, \Delta \, d$, that is, the price in relation to the change in quantity, divided by the quantity with respect to the price change. In the MC equation $p \, \Delta \, q$ equals p, and $q \, \Delta \, p$ equals the variable cost of a single unit with respect to its price. When $e > 1$, the MC is rising; when $e = 1$, the MC is unchanged; and when $e < 1$, the MC is declining.

Marginal outlay is the buyer's cost of persuading the seller to sell one more unit. The marginal outlay includes the buyer's variable cost, which is the change of price, increasing or decreasing, in response to the demand. Marginal outlay can be stated thus: $MO = p + VC$. The buyer's elasticity is also p/VC; at the time of the sales transaction the price paid must equal the price agreed upon by the seller, so that $[MC = MO] \equiv MR$ is an identity relationship that must always hold for the doctrine of Marginalism.

This of course means that $(p - VC)_s = (p + VC)_b$, with the subscripts standing for seller and buyer. Since $e = p/VC$ for both sides of the transaction, the MC and MO equations can be written thus: $(p - p/e)_s \equiv (p + p/e)_b$. From this identity derived from the above equations some unwanted consequences can be drawn.

For example, by setting the elasticities to unity, the identity takes the form $0p_s \equiv 2p_b$; this is clearly not the case, for a price does exist at which the transaction was made, in which the seller's and buyer's prices were equal. If the elasticity of one side is greater or lesser than the other, adjustments will be made until the transaction is completed or until it is abandoned. Equal elasticities, either greater or lesser than unity, result in similar difficulties, rendering different prices for the sale and purchase when in fact only one price is set for the transaction.

This difficulty represents a clash between situational logic, in this case the logic of Marginalism, and reality. According to Marginal reasoning such a transaction price is set according to the marginal propensities to sell and consume, and on this point there is no clash. The difficulty comes when this price setting is derived from Marginalism and results in a paradox of no transaction price according to the derivation and a real transaction price by which commerce is undertaken. The paradox does not exist because of the reality but because of Marginalist logic.

This difficulty can be resolved by applying the utility approach. The seller sets the product's price, taking into account his costs and an acceptable profit rate within the framework of competition and his client's ability to pay. Hence, the price represents the acceptable utility of the product as assessed by the seller. The buyer considers the seller's costs and his profit mark-up, knowing that he cannot obtain the product at the seller's cost and must calculate his own expected utility from the purchase, translating this utility into the price he agrees to pay.

The buyer may accept the seller's price, in which case his expected utility is translated into actual utility bringing both utilities into equality as determined by the price. Moreover, the buyer's utility is in accordance with the seller's utility assessment at the time of the transaction, so that before the transaction, should the buyer bargain to reduce the seller's price, and should the seller agree, then the new price is within the acceptable limits of utility set by the seller, and indeed he most likely calculated the chances of bargaining before the original price was set. In all instances, then, at the time of transaction, the identity is $(pf(p/u))_s \equiv T\,(pf(p/u))_b$ since the p/u's for both sides have the same value at transaction time T and the seller's and buyer's price at the time of transaction are equal and functions of their utilities, then the identity holds and the reality corresponds to the results derived from the utility theorem.

Another difficulty with Marginalism concerns the marginal efficiency of capital (MEC) employed by Keynes in *The General Theory*. This is the relationship between the prospective yield of a capital asset and its supply price. The prospective yield of an asset, such as an investment, is the series of annuities $Q_1, Q_2, \cdots, Q_n$ that the investor expects to gain from selling the investment's output after expenses are deducted. The asset's supply price is, not its market price, but that price which would induce manufacturers or borrowers to produce an additional asset unit; this is sometimes referred to as the replacement cost.

Keynes defines the MEC as being equal to the rate of discount that would make the present value of the series of annuities given by the returns expected from the capital asset during its life just equal to the supply price—its replacement cost.[8] Because the MEC depends on the rate of return expected to be on money as if it were a newly produced asset, that is, a measure, neglected is the historical result of the asset's yield on its original cost if looked at after the asset's life has ended.

From this a paradox can be constructed. Let $M(\text{MEC}X)_{t_a} - {}_{t_c}$ stand for the market value of an asset expected to have the MEC of X over the life span of time a to c. If during this period only a few purchases of the asset are purchased, its MEC from the investors' points of view is affected insignificantly, a fact judged with considerable accuracy, so that the real rate of return on the investment is that which is expected. Here there is no problem.

If, however, during the period a to c a large investment is realized in the asset, the MEC will decline accordingly. Let this be represented by $M(\text{MEC-}X)$, where $-X$ is the MEC of X lower than the MEC for its first investor and existing in time b. Thus,

$$M(\text{MEC}X)_{t_a} - {}_{t_c} \neq M(\text{MEC}X)_{t_a} - {}_{t_c}$$

because during this time span the expected yield of X was lowered in reality to $-X$, so that the logical construction of the MEC over time results in the paradox of not being the MEC over the same period of time.

It may be argued that the reasoning here is unfair, that what must be considered is the entire investment schedule, which would show the aggregate increase in investment and the appropriate decline in the asset's MEC. This is certainly what Keynes meant when he cautioned against the confusion the MEC has brought about because we fail to understand that it depends on the *prospective* yield and not its current yield.

> This can be best illustrated by pointing out the effect on the marginal efficiency of capital of an expectation of changes in the prospective cost of production, whether these changes are expected to come from changes in labour cost, *i.e.*, in the wage-unit, or from inventions and new technique.... In so far as such developments are foreseen as probable, or even as possible, the marginal efficiency of capital produced to-day is appropriately diminished.[9]

In the real world where most things are probable if not possible, it may very well be that an investor does not foresee any changes and that the investor's personal expectation of the MEC is held constant, while others who have invested in the same asset have experienced a decline in the MEC. In any case, the investment-demand schedule will be altered in reality whether such an alteration is expected or not. Keynes's point, instead of clarifying the confusion, only emphasizes it.

This paradox can be resolved, however, with the application of utility. The constriction in which the MEC over time is not the MEC over time because expectations were not realized can be approached from the utility position. When the MEC is replaced with utility, the role of expectation remains strictly personal and psychological and is not included in the asset's actual utility. Granted that the total of expectation is the basis on which the investment was made for the projected yield over time, but this expectation may or may not correspond to the asset's utility. There is therefore no paradox, for expected and actual utilities must be kept separate. Thus,

$$[M(u^X_{t_a} - {}_{t_c} \equiv M(u^X_{t_a} - {}_{t_c}] \text{ if and only if } [u_{t_a} - {}_{t_c} \equiv u_{t_a} - {}_{t_c}].$$

Where $E/uX = uX$, that is, where the expected utility is equal to the actual utility, then the expectation is confirmed in reality; where $E/uX \neq uX$ over the time period, say in time b, then the expectation is not realized and only the actual utility should be considered. Keeping expectations separate from utility eliminates the difficulty of the MEC.

The trouble with Marginalism is that it seeks to objectify the subjective aspect of expectation. This was shown in the first argument given, where the differing elasticities of buyer and seller were attributed to the subjective perspectives of the parties to the bargaining process. The second argument illustrates this by showing that the decline of the MEC is due to a difference between subjective expectation and the objective reality in which the asset is regarded. Utility combines expectation with reality, both with their measurements; they affect each other, but expectation and reality are kept separate because of the requirements of utility.

5

ON MONEY, INTEREST, AND PRICES

GENERAL REMARKS

In his discussion on the theory of prices Keynes stated that the importance of money is due essentially to its being a strong link between the present and the future. Taking this point further, it can be seen that money's importance is due to its being the link between the past and the future. Just as the past contained a specific and historically unique set of circumstances that determined the purchasing power of money, today's events and those of the future are the factors that are the determinants of the power of money within the specific existing historical conditions.

Nevertheless, the function of money, its socioeconomic purpose, remains constant over time regardless of the historical circumstances. Money serves as a means of exchange; savings programs and investment opportunities that provide for monetary renumeration at a fixed and future date in return for risk taking and abstention of use are sophisticated refinements of the means-of-exchange function that money plays in society.

Although the function of money remains constant and saving and investing provide economic growth and sociological development in politically stable societies, the historical differences of events that determine the purchasing power of money cannot be overlooked. The uses of money have led to the search for common denominators as a basis for curtailing too-rapid economic expansion and too severe a slowing down of economic activity. The economist today searches for historical situations similar to our current worldwide recession. Since the current period has no precedent other than the Great Depression, economists seek similarities between these two periods of historical economic crisis and analyze once again the theories that led to the easing of the crisis of the past to determine their merits in relating to our current historical situation.

During the Great Depression, as now, the problem was both institutional and theoretical. Institutionally, large amounts of productive capital equipment were lying idle while unemployment was high. This is the situation now. However, then the currencies were so deflated that major attempts by private industry to retool for new production programs were unprofitable and the necessary investment from the private sector was not forthcoming. The institutional problem was getting industry in motion to absorb the unproductive labor force and generate demand through increased production and general increased liquidity in the form of wages. Keynes offered the advice of placing people in jobs, doing whatever tasks could be found, and thus giving them purchasing power through income. Aggregate increased purchasing power would put pressure on industry for increasing its inventories, which in turn would require an adequate labor force for stocking these inventories. Recovery would set in and the depression would be eliminated, with the newly injected money resulting in reemployment and a work force capable of investing, purchasing, and bringing the economy to a healthy condition.

To accomplish this revival, Keynes advocated that the government become an active participant in economic affairs; he thus revolutionized the institutional basis of economics. Before *The General Theory*, the solutions offered for solving the Great Depression were steeped in the *laissez-faire* doctrine, established economically by Adam Smith and rooted politically in the teachings of Thomas Jefferson, in which for both economic and political affairs the government that governs best governs least. This was an ideological imposition accepted by the neoclassicists—a position that prohibited them from taking the bold and necessary step of advocating an active yet limited role for government in economics to provide the basis for recovery. Hence, the neoclassical thinkers varied their explanations of the crisis and based their proposed solutions around the themes of restricted economic activity: Either the government restricts economic activity through too much interference in the workings of the market or the unions restrict labor mobility and fix artificial wage levels and thereby prevent market forces from determining the wage and price levels necessary for securing the employment levels required for maintaining efficient resource allocation, or on both the government and the unions at varying degrees.

In *The General Theory* Keynes commented on several of these arguments. He devoted much time to the serious argument of A. C. Pigou's theory of unemployment. He respected Pigou's theory, describing it as the most comprehensive analysis of neoclassical theory; yet he criticized it for not recognizing the unstable factor of investment, significant in the fluctuation in employment but neglected as such by the neoclassicists. This neoclassical failure of recognition was responsible for the doctrine that cyclic fluctuations are "natural" in capitalist economies. The mechanism of fluctuation was the level of inventories; as they were depleted, so the theory goes, a state of depression would exist until new demand for goods and services would require retooling and restocking; as inventories were replenished to the point of saturation, employment would decline and prices would eventually decline until stocks could be moved and retooling begin anew; leading to restocking of inventories and reemployment to meet the demand for replenishing inventories. This mechanistic argument failed to consider that goods and services would always be moved, no matter how slow the rate, but that retooling and restocking of inventories depend on reinvestment, which if at insignificant levels, would not bring the cycle out of its depressed condition.

This indeed was the case Keynes argued. Uncertainty over the market situation and the state of the economy prohibited the necessary funds from being injected to stimulate industrial output that would allow old inventories to move and new inventories to be accumulated. Innovations that could generate new markets were kept at extremely low levels because investments to finance them were slow in coming. Products with low profit margins were phased out, increasing the unemployment level and reducing demand still further through the decline in consumer liquidity. The obvious conclusion, yet one that seemed to conflict with political considerations, was drawn out by Keynes when he advocated that if the private sector would not nor could not provide the investments sufficient to move the cycle upward, the public sector, that is, the government, had to undertake the investment to increase aggregate liquidity for retooling and restocking of inventories, thereby generating demand and establishing renewed confidence in the economy.

The theoretical problem Keynes dealt with was the difficulty of formulating an economic theory that not only would explain the reasons for the Great Depression but also would provide a basis of reasoning that would solve the crisis and establish guidelines for institutional, that is, governmental, decision making in light of further economic fluctuations. This Keynes sought in his treatment of money, interest, and employment. He attacked the theoretical basis of employment as merely a function of the supply and demand for labor and criticized Say's Law as the philosophical foundation for this reasoning. Keynes formulated his theory emphasizing investment and saving as the monetary sources for industrial activity and hence for employment, thereby giving credence to his institutional argument that if such investment is not forthcoming by the private sector, then only the public sector can bear the responsibility for maintaining economic activity through stimulating and contributing to investment. Hence, Keynes showed that the institutional and theoretical problems are inseparable, that policy must be related to theory, and that the theory must be such as to yield appropriate decision-making policy for the situation.

Keynes stated another methodological point, that a theory is relevant only for its specific conditions. He argued this in the beginning of *The General Theory*, where in the very brief first chapter he wrote, "I shall argue that the postulates of the neoclassical theory are applicable to a special case only and not to the general case, the situation it assumes being a limiting point of the possible positions of equilibrium."[1] Indeed, similarities between situations must be recognized for what they are and not as identities. Seeking points of comparison between the Great Depression and the present economic crisis can yield instructive guidelines but not identical prescriptions nor cures. The most obvious common factors are idle capital and unemployment. Then, however, there was deflation; now, high inflation. Then, the banks and exchange markets were outside the regulation of governing bodies; today, they are very much regulated and subject to government control. Indeed, even Keynes's dictum that the government should assume an active role to stimulate investment, maintain interest rates, and contribute to aggregate consumer liquidity, while sound advice for an economy in depression seeking money to move the cycle upward, Keynes's dictum is most questionable now. Keynes's theoretical contributions concerning money and interest must be replaced by theorems relevant to the contemporary economic situation, for the theory of economics Keynes stated is appropriate only for the special conditions of the crisis with which he dealt.

ON MONEY AND LIQUIDITY

In his discussion on prices Keynes commented that some economists concerned with the theory of value who teach that prices are determined by supply and demand and on the elasticities of short-run supply and changes in marginal costs with respect to demand very quickly lapse into jargon when discussing the theory of money and prices, embarking on discourses of the velocity of income, time changes, the quantity theory of money, and every other concept that can possibly be associated with it. While Keynes's comment is valid, he did not mention the reasons for it. In its broadest sense a theory of value must pertain to the relationship between money and the goods and services money can purchase. This concerns the relationship between consumption and prices and the analysis of the elasticities of supply and demand during short- and long-run fluctuations as well as changes in wages. This must also take into account the quantity of the money supply, the level of savings and investments, and the current government fiscal and monetary policies and the manner which these policies affect the other factors, as well as the available quantities of goods and services acquirable through monetary transactions.

In his chapter on prices, Keynes formulated a Velocity Theory of Money from which price elasticities, output, wages, and employment could be determined. This is not an association of loosely connected concepts but a theory that allows for a process of derivation, hence overcoming that very criticism he leveled against other economists. His formula is $MV = D$, where M is the quantity of money, V is its income-velocity, the value of which is dependent on the institutional factors of banking, on social habits, on the social income distribution, and on the effective cost of holding cash as opposed to investing–itself determined by the available personal holdings and by the interest rate. Earlier, Keynes defined money as consisting of two parts: M_1 for precautionary holdings and transactions; M_2 for the amount held for speculative motives. Hence, $(M_1 + M_2)V = D$. D is the effective demand for money as determined by these components of money and its income-velocity, which is a social and an institutional component of the equation.

Further, $M = L_1(Y) - L_2(r)$, with L being the liquidity function so that $L_1(Y)$ is the income function and $L_2(r)$ is the interest-rate function. Substituting L for M in the Velocity Theory shows that velocity at which money circulates is equal to the effective demand for goods and services, both functions of income and the interest rate.

From his formula Keynes derives the elasticities of employment, wages, output, and demand, keeping true to his claim that he joined a quantity theory of money to elasticity. This he did by differentiating each factor with respect to the standard elasticity equation, so that elasticity $e = Ddp/pdD$, and so forth. Elasticity is a micro concept while the velocity of money is a macro concept, and this micro-macro dichotomy remains in Keynes's treatment. He could not remove this dichotomy because, as he maintained, money is the economic connection between the past and the present; elasticities show only short-run movement while the effects of the money supply and its velocity of circulation are long run and concern investment and liquidity that cannot be measured by elasticity but must be considered from a different view.

This dichotomy can be resolved, however, by the formula $M = Y$, that is, by equating the money in the economy to the national income. Y is broken into three components: $Y = Y_p + Y_g + Y_f$. The Y_p corresponds to Keynes's M_1 and M_2; that is, it is money for personal transactions and precautions such as sound savings and investments in the form of government bonds and blue-chip shares; these are programs in which only marginal risks are involved and dividends are paid according to the demand for money for these investments and savings and in relation to the demand for other investment and savings programs. Included in this classification is speculation in which both the risks and the remuneration on investments are high. The Y_p (personal income) is derived from wages, inheritance, profits on investments, and other money sources at the individual's disposal. The Y_g, income generated by the government, is that income which the government has at its disposal as a result of tax collection, payments on loans from foreign countries, gains from bond purchases, and grants from foreign countries and international monetary bodies, a factor of significance for the lesser developed countries. The Y_f, the firm's income, is the net profits from the firm's business transactions, monies from government grants and loans and from funding from nongovernment sources, monies from stock and bond issues, and liquidity gained from mergers.

As $M = Y$, then $M_p = Y_p$, and $M_g = Y_g$, and $M_f = Y_f$. This formulation leads very easily to a value theory relating the micro aspects of price changes to the macro aspect of the velocity of money (recall that the value theory is based on utility and entropy, as stated in the last chapter). In Keynes's $MV = D$ equation, if the velocity of money is constant, changes in price will be proportional to changes in the money supply, providing that the change with respect to demand is unity; this notion of elasticity explains the situation after the price changes and provides no guidance concerning the dynamics of such changes. However, for the $M = Y$ equation, part of the money in the economy, that is, part of the Y component, will be held as liquid assets; this is liquidity not in circulation, so that the equation can be written $M = Y_c + Y_d$, with Y_c being money that is in circulation and Y_d being money withheld from circulation. The Y_d is the liquidity element and hold for personal disposable income, income held by firms and the government that has not been used for investment. It is to this liquidity that the value theory must apply.

This is because all changes in prices, wages, output, and employment affect the liquidity preference. Upward price changes bring about a lower disposable national income and hence a reduced short-term liquidity expressed in altered and then stable demand. This upward price movement has a short-term effect on wages, output, and employment that is even more significant in the medium and long run when disposable income is further reduced and the liquidity preference altered by the multiplying effects of inflation. Unless wages are adjusted upward so that the value of disposable income has the same expected utility as before, output will be affected by labor unrest, with the consequent decline in employment as efforts are made to maintain the present wage level. When the existing wage structure or even an increased structure for the same level of employment is maintained, unemployment, being larger in its seasonal and frictional levels will result in inflation because of the competing consumer disposable income for the same goods and services. The value of disposable income will then decline along with the decline in liquidity because a greater proportion of income is required for consumption. Also, the quantity of goods and services will decline because of unemployment and the reduced managerial programs of innovation and imitation inspired by the firms' cautious outlook.

In contrast, an overall decrease in the general price level will result in an increase in the value of disposable income, with firms becoming more indulgent, engaging in more projects to increase the aggregate profit levels. Either a steady rate or an increased rate of investments will result, affecting the borrower's interest rates. Price reductions are due in part to increased competition that increases consumer liquidity; lower prices with high rates of disposable income increase liquidity that can be channeled into investment or increased consumption.

Apart from offering price reductions, industry may be unable to exploit this increased liquidity because of market uncertainty and the unknown effect the change in the value of money may have on interest rates and opportunities for introducing new projects as well as because of uncertainty concerning consumer response to the expansion of existing and hitherto successful programs. There are two reasons for this. One is that since the end of the Great Depression, the government has maintained an extensive role in economic affairs, establishing a reliance of industry on government. Industry's hesitance to carry out projects during times of uncertainty is thus due in part to waiting for government action and observing the consequences of such action when it does come. Therefore—and the second reason—the difficulty of initiating projects is compounded by the time lag between the action and the consequences of this action, expected or otherwise.

A program of injecting more money into the economy requires a period of time before the consequences of this injection are felt. Greater industrial liquidity, one possible consequence, may not lead to the government's desired result of greater industrial activity; it may instead result in managers holding this liquidity until the markets are ready to absorb new and different products. The added liquidity at the consumers' disposal may not go into further purchases, thus signaling the clearing of the markets, but may go to pay off debts incurred or into investing as a hedge against further uncertainty.

During periods of inflationary pressure governments will act to reduce the money supply and, through the banks, to reduce credit, thus reducing the money available for further borrowing and industrial expansion. Consumption will then decline to a level that should signal industry to cut back on production and postpone plans for introducing new products. Whether this signal is acknowledged or appreciated depends, of course, on the individual firms' competitive positions. A firm can, for example, increase its own liquidity during periods of decreasing macro liquidity by altering the gearing ratio and by offering better terms to those institutional lenders willing to invest in spite of the macro restrictions. The successful firms thus are able to cover a greater proportion of their markets while their competitors either maintain their present output or cut back because their cost-pricing policies do not allow sufficient profit margins to maintain production levels. Another advantage of offering good terms on loans and achieving greater liquidity during uncertain times is that such policies allow for research into innovative and imitative projects, thereby maintaining the employment of skilled labor while other firms seek to safeguard their profit positions by the short-run measure of reducing their wage payments.

However, as uncertainty deepens and firms are inclined to reduce their business activities, they exert an influence on the money supply. The velocity of circulation decreases and effective demand necessarily declines. With the recession, firms will merge to preserve their positions, and a reordering of priorities will result. Those firms that retain their identities will phase out marginally profitable products and forestall initiating innovative and imitative projects, with the purpose of maintaining their present profit levels with respect to their total costs.

Since, as the equation states, money equals that part of income in circulation and that part not yet introduced into the economic system, the velocity of money in circulation is a function of its utility, that is, $V_M = u(M)$. The consumer's budget is broken down into transactions accounting for purchases made and debts paid, as well as for disposable income for savings and investments; this second category, disposable income, determines the consumer's liquidity ratio that although earmarked for investments and savings can be recalled for consumption within a time stipulated by the terms of the portfolio. Firms account for that part of money allocated for consumption but vie for the remainder, which is the disposable income. Consumers judge how to spend their money on the basis of their utility ordering. And since the velocity of money is a function of utility, firms seek to formulate their projects to achieve the highest appeal to their prospective consumers.

Note that this point was indicated by Marris when he discussed his pioneering and sheeplike consumers. It must be emphasized that these roles are not economically nor sociologically fixed and rigid. They depend on the product, on the circumstances of its market exposure, and on the geographical location of potential consumers.

Nor is there any paradox here. Investments and savings are means by which firms acquire liquidity. Should they attract a sufficient level of consumer patronage, their reliance on outside investors and savers would decrease and their financing would be strictly internal, by means of accepting lower per-product profit and higher aggregate liquidity, or by other means of maneuvering.

This theory, however, has been proved to be utopian, and the firms must cope with the consumers' aggregate utility rating. Although the individual consumer may calculate that his money has greater utility if closed in savings and investment or may diversify and increase both investments and consumption, the managers of the firms must relate to the aggregate utility function as it affects the velocity of money in circulation; they must thus seek to increase their profits through offering products that will attract attention and place high on consumers' utility ratings.

The money-income equation can be stated another way: $M = (L\epsilon)Y$, which means that money is equal to income of which liquidity is a component. Liquidity is derived from the use of money, such as from wages and returns on investments and savings programs. This liquidity, expressed as disposable income, is transferred into working money in the form of investments and savings that are loaned and receive interest or in the form of purchases, in which case the money directed toward consumption goes into meeting costs and profits. Liquidity as disposable income must therefore be included in national income because it is a factor to which projects are constructed and advertising directed. Although it is money not yet used, it stimulates economic activity to absorb it. Hence, the extent of liquidity also depends on the level of income—a factor determined by the price level.

From this argument, $V_M = u(M)$ and $M = Y$, the velocity of money is a function of the utility of money and of national income. Because velocity depends on utility, the theory of value is a utility theory; it determines which products will be consumed and which types of projects managers should strive to innovate and more specifically imitate if the markets for these products have already been pioneered. Because the velocity of money is a function of income of which disposable liquidity income is a component, the rate at which money moves within the economy depends on the rate at which disposable income is placed in the economy, either through direct consumption or indirectly through savings and investments. The preference for holding money for interest or in exchange for goods and services determines its velocity; this preference is the expression of utility rating. Hence, contrary to Keynes's approach, the value of money here is an expression of the theory of value as a utility concept, making possible a choice between holding money either as liquid or exchanging it for goods and services. This makes possible individual utility preferences, thereby giving rise to an aggregate utility ordering that can be tapped through innovation and imitation.

THE INTEREST RATE

How does this utility theory of value apply to the interest rate? Historically, classical and neoclassical economists have held that the interest rate is that rate which equates the supply of money with the demand for money, for either short-term or long-term liquidity, so that at any one moment in time the macro supply and demand for money is held in equilibrium by the interest rate. Keynes pointed out that the interest rate is not a magic instrument for keeping the economy or its money supply in balance; it is a part of the macro economy that cannot be examined validly in isolation. Keynes explained the interest rate in terms of liquidity, with the preference of holding liquid assets as an inverse determinant to the interest rate. The higher the interest rate, the lower the amount of liquid money; the lower the interest rate, the greater the liquidity.

In his chapter on the theory of interest Keynes stated a functional relationship, $M = L(r)$, that is, money is a liquidity-preference function of the interest rate r; he comments that this relationship explains how the quantity of money enters the economic scheme. A high rate of interest brings about a decline in disposable income because the money is saved and invested to reap the high rate of return. Keynes maintained that this results in at least stable demand while the money acquired through the high interest rate (reflecting its scarcity at that rate) is used to generate production. The mechanism is such that with demand sufficiently stable, the newly increased aggregate supply of goods and services resulting from the new production reduces aggregate prices, which leads soon after to increased consumption. Interest rates decline accordingly as the demand for money for industrial expansion falls with expansion financed by sales earnings, and not from borrowing and money is released for increasing consumption and liquidity. This continues until inventories begin to approach depletion and the demand for money for replenishing stocks increases; the result is that the interest rate rises again as the firms compete for this liquidity. This system is one of movement around a general equilibrium position, for money is either saved and invested or held liquid as disposable income, depending on the economy's requirements.

As Keynes wrote during the Great Depression, he recognized that this system was not infallible and that as a consequence of its breaking down, the government had to take measures initiating manifold and diversified projects to inject money into the economy—money that had the backing of employment and output to maintain its value. Potential demand would then be converted to effective demand as purchases increased, placing pressure on industry to retool and restock, with money then being absorbed by the interest rate, thus maintaining inflation at a reasonable rate after the seriously deflated period.

The problem that exists now is, however, one of serious inflation and not that of the deflation that existed at the time Keynes wrote; his approach to the interest rate is geared to reviving consumption through converting potential to effective demand. Our contemporary situation is unique in that the preference to hold liquidity is not being aligned with the industrial demand for money by being regulated by the interest rate, so that instead of production being at the level where aggregate demand brings about reduced or stable prices according to production costs and profit margins, production has to compete with investment and the consumer's profit considerations as to how his money is to be used.[2]

Of course, Keynes's point that the nature of the interest rate can be understood only within the context of macroeconomics is still valid. The difference today is that the nature of the interest rate itself has changed in accordance with the changing economic situation. To clarify its macroeconomic function, consider the interest rate's role in microeconomics.

The firm considers the interest rate as the return on investments that can viably attract funds from being used for other purposes; thus, the interest rate is the rate of return calculated by management for attracting these funds for project financing. The rate of return from the managerial position is based on projected production and distribution costs, advertising expenditures, and taxes, thereby allowing for the return on investments to be included in the overall costing but not included in profits. The rate of return should be attractive enough to compete with other firms and sources vying for this liquidity, with the projected inflation rate considered as a factor in this calculation. Computation must be such that the rate offered is competitive yet sufficiently low so as not to affect the firm's operations through repayment.[3]

In his *Treatise on Money* Keynes defined what he called the natural rate of interest as being that rate which preserves the equality between the rates of savings and investments. In *The General Theory*, however, he argued that this definition was an attempt to clarify Wicksell's position and that as each society has a different set of rates, the concept of the natural rate is no longer useful (cited from *The General Theory*, p. 242). However, the point is surely not that each society has its own set of interest rates between savings and investments that can be unified statistically and that fluctuates in response to the macro conditions and the changing politicoeconomic world situation. Should a global interest rate be determined, it may be useful to the econometrician seeking to find internal economic activity and the flow of liquidity among the various economies. But the significant point of the interest rate is that for each investment opportunity the rate of return at which the investment is made reflects the investment's utility as considered by the managerial board in its planning, costing, and bargaining for available funds, as well as by the investor's individual utility preference. If a natural rate of interest exists, it reflects the actual utilities for savings and investments and for holding liquidity as determined by individuals who place their monies in various programs and managers who construct these programs. The econometrician, examining the statistically derived global interest rate, could draw general conclusions about capital flows and the internal macro utility of money within each economy; for these conclusions to have practical relevance, however, it is necessary to examine on the micro level each proposal for investment and the corresponding conversion of liquidity to investment to draw rigorous conclusions from this study.

Thus, what must be considered by both management and the potential investor is the investment's utility. From management's position the utility is assessed by the product's potential success as determined by its costing and expected returns projected by market research. The investor, however, must consider alternative sources for investment or hold liquidity; he must diversify his portfolios to ensure the highest obtainable rate of return, calculating the proposed interest rates offered by competing alternatives against the risk involved in the investment. The utility rate of interest is that rate of return offered by management to the investor after allocations are made. It is the rate which is accepted by the investor for placing his money after he considers the most profitable investments and the trade-off between holding liquidity and portfolios.

No economic mystique surrounds the utility rate of interest. It is unlike Wicksell's natural rate of interest, which determines the equilibrium rate for investments and projects. It fluctuates according to the utility placed on it by investors and managers. If economic activity tends to slow down and if money is scarce and in demand, the utility of money will increase and the interest rates on aggregate will rise. These rates tend to fall if managers reduce the number of projects presented to investors, thus reducing the utility of money. Should the demand for money due to increased activity exceed supply, the utility of investing will increase as the interest rates rise to acquire money for the firms. While sufficient liquidity is absorbed the interest rate tends to decline as the utility for holding money by the firms declines, thereby releasing liquidity as disposable income, partially set aside for consumption. However, it must be stressed that these movements are tendencies and no necessity is implied. Interest rates may, for example, decline during the initial stages of economic activity as firms use idle liquidity already at their disposal, thereby eliminating the need to pay interest on borrowed funds. During periods of declining activity interest rates may increase as firms may seek liquidity for realizing projects when the slowdown ends and thus acquire liquidity at lower rates. The utility of money and the interest rate depends on specific circumstances and the personal orderings of preference and does not depend on economic "mechanics."

Contrary to the utility rate of interest, the natural and neutral rates of interest—the latter is said to exist during periods of full employment[4] —are strictly macroeconomic and equilibrium oriented. They are mechanically based on the de facto functions and tend to be self-regulatory, like Smith's "invisible hand" regulating the markets when each person acts in self-interest. The natural rate of interest in this view is supposed to correspond to that aspect of the "invisible hand" that regulates the supply and demand for loanable funds, maintaining these factors in equilibrium. However, were such equilibrium indeed operating, there would be no serious problem with these factors, for macroequilibrium approaches such as the Harrod-Domar model could be employed, keeping the economy on an equilibrium growth path.

The utility rate of interest is not intended as a balancing force between the supply and demand for loanable funds but depends on each project for the liquidity of each investor. The investment transaction will be made at an interest rate set by the investor's acceptance of the project's utility and by management's offering the rate according to its demand for money and the prospective sales and profits derivable from the project.

How is this utility rate of interest to be computed? In *The General Theory* Keynes stated a formula for the computation of the interest rate. He argued that if ldr is the value in the present of £ deferred for r years and it is known that ndr will be the value of £1 in the year n for n deferred years, then $ndr = ldn + r/ldn$. He stated further that if the future rates of interest are uncertain, there is no necessary reason why this equation should hold. It is understood that a degree of uncertainty always exists in economic activity, with the best of plans influenced by forces unexpected and uncontrollable by individuals and firms. Nevertheless, given our contemporary system of managerial economics, the interest-rate computation must be revised. Some degree of certainty can be found in our uncertain world.

Managerial considerations relate not only to planning and executing production but also to financial matters such as returns paid on investments as well as investors' considerations as to the use of their liquidity. The interest-rate computation must be revised, becoming $E/U(idnr/ldn)$, with E/U being that part of utility expected from the investor's and the management's sides. It is when this expectation on both sides is equal that the investment is made, with the rest of the formula determining the rate of return to be offered.

Before placing their money investors must compute their expected utilities, ordering them according to their understanding of the possibilities available and their desired rate of return on their investment. The managers have their own computations regarding the rate of return they are able to pay for the use of money. The investors' computations take into account the objective market conditions and realities while the management's calculations are based on projected and analyzed models of future market dynamics. When the investors' objective and expected utility reach agreement with the expected and objective utility established by management, the investment is made at the set rate at contracted terms—at the interest rate *r*. Should these utilities not be in agreement for both sides of the transaction, the liquidity will not be absorbed by the interest rate until one or both sides alter their utility ordering. Hence no mechanism is involved in maintaining equilibrium because the interest rate is based on the subjective and objective utility considerations manifested in bargaining. There may be the extreme case where high interest rates are offered but investors prefer to hold their money liquid because no economic necessity exists dictating that objective utility should overcome expected utility ordering. The utility preferences of each investor cannot be economically quantified; although when investments are made, the interest rate signifies the utility of the investment, equating both the objective and subjective components in each side of the bargaining process.

In contemporary economics there is movement among projects, some being phased out while others are developed. This is a manifestation of the profit motive expressed by the utility of investment and production, of choosing liquidity or returns on money in light of new projects offering acceptable interest rates. In a dynamic disequilibrium economy transferring of disposable income into investments continues as long as the utility of doing so remains. Once the utility is undermined by either or both sides, the relationship begins to break down and entropy sets in. In an economy in which the dynamic processes of growth are maintained, investments are rescheduled and projects are phased out while others are initiated. Should management falter in the aggregate, employment and prices are affected, with inflation chasing after goods and services reduced in quantity by reduced production and unemployment. As is the case now, inflation with near stagnation are the consequences. This is further discussed later in an analysis of the process of recession in the managerial economy in which are suggested remedies for revitalizing the economy.

6
THE DYNAMICS OF THE CONTEMPORARY FIRM

COMMENTS ON SCHUMPETER'S THEORY: BACKGROUND INFORMATION

In Chapter 4 the role of the contemporary manager as described in the literature was discussed with regard to innovation and imitation. In that chapter this role as presented in managerial theory was determined inadequate, for the role must be expanded to approach innovation and imitation in a manner suitable to the present crisis and not merely to the economics of firms the theory developed since World War II. Although this accepted theory is important, it has proven itself inadequate for setting guidelines dealing with the problems of stagnation and inflation in their present proportions. The foundation of contemporary managerial capitalism was provided by Schumpeter and his contribution must be discussed briefly.

In his work *The Theory of Economic Development*, Schumpeter placed dynamism of economic growth and development in the hands of the entrepreneur. It is the entrepreneur who innovates in business by carrying out new combinations in business activity that break the flow of existing patterns, so that the entrepreneur swims against the tide. This definition, Schumpeter maintained, corresponds to Say's definition of the entrepreneur as that person who musters together productive factors and combines them into a working profitable structure. There is agreement with Say, but Schumpeter's work goes much further.

Schumpeter's book first appeared in English at the appropriate date of 1934, in the midst of the Great Depression. He wrote the book in the beginning of the twentieth century, having formulated his ideas as early as 1907, with the German edition appearing in 1911. He had the advantage of considering Say's argument and those of the neoclassical writers in light of Say's reasoning.

Say's argument is that once the entrepreneur musters together resources to begin a business and starts and maintains it successfully, entrepreneurial activity ceases. Schumpeter agreed with Say on the necessity of the entrepreneur to muster these resources successfully in a viable business, but he maintained that this is only part of the task, for entrepreneurial activity requires breaking the economic flow and going against established economic patterns. Thus, what was formerly a help becomes a hinderance. What was familiar datum becomes an unknown. Where the boundaries of routine stop, many people can go no further, and the rest can do so only "in an highly variable manner."[1] By going against the tide the entrepreneur brings into the market a new product, which–if successful commercially–reaps a short-run gain, to be reduced and eliminated by imitators and by the returns on the investments to be paid to the capitalist backers who supported the project. After the successes of the entrepreneurial activity the innovating businessperson often loses the character of the entrepreneur and settles down to normal activity: "This is the rule, of course, and hence it is just as rare for anyone always to remain an entrepreneur throughout the decades of his active life as it is for a businessman never to have a moment in which he is an entrepreneur, to however a modest degree."[2] Hence, Schumpeter's entrepreneur has two distinct and necessary tasks. First, the entrepreneur amasses capital to finance his idea, seeking the most money at the lowest possible interest rate to reduce his risk in the project. Second, after having financial backing, the entrepreneur breaks into the economic flow and brings his product to the attention of consumers.

The entrepreneur, for Schumpeter, is most likely already established in business, which allows him sufficient collateral to obtain financial backing at terms favorable to him. He is probably operating at a break-even production level; and because he dedicates his time and the productive capacity of his established business to his current project, his current production most likely suffers reductions and the established business takes a loss. The entrepreneur's competitors tend to view him askance, as a gambler willing to take risks at the expense of his current production; the more he is suspect, the greater the difficulty in swimming against the economic tide.

Should the entrepreneur not already be in business, his project would be that much more difficult to undertake. Backers would be less willing to support the project, and those who do provide financial backing ensure compensation at high interest and demand heavy collateral in case of failure.

In either case, the entrepreneur's profits are short lived as imitators move into the profitable market with close substitutions. The entrepreneur who lacks an already-established business would feel the hurt most because his short-lived profits would be wiped out through competition and he lacks the infrastructure to give him support. The innovative product, if successful, brings about alterations in the economic flow as imitators diversify and rechannel resources into producing close substitutes, at the expense of already-existing products whose profits have become marginal through competition.

THE SCHEMATIC OF THE CONTEMPORARY FIRM

The present situation of managerial and government-managed economics has altered radically the entrepreneurial role of innovation and that of imitation. This does not mean that Schumpeter's description of economic development is totally irrelevant, for it does operate on a local level in the community where the bold entrepreneur resides. This form of innovation, however, has no impact on the macro economy. This discussion must therefore be focused on the type of firm that does influence the economy and is in turn influenced by the dynamics it generates and by the dynamics of other firms in competition. In Schumpeter's economy no business is large enough to control sufficient resources to be able to engage in both innovation and imitation; the contemporary firm, however, has achieved the bigness and diversification to exercise these options.

In order to clarify the dynamics of the firm with respect to innovation and imitation, a static picture must be first presented, after which the firm's dynamics can be explored. The term F_t stands for the firm in time t. The firm's general economic position is represented by its supply-and-demand relationship expressed by the equation $F_t = S \cup D$, with the union sign $\cup$ indicating that part of the total market capacity represented by the firm's activities. The supply position is that which the firm has acquired in its diversified market activity, indicating the products it manufactures and distributes. The demand position is the sum total of the customers who purchase and use the firm's goods and services in time t. Since the sum total of the firms in an economy make up the aggregate macro supply and demand, the supply and demand structures differ with each firm at any one time. This necessary difference is manifested in managerial attempts at innovation and "invading" the territories of other firms through imitation.

A firm's utility for its production programs is computed with respect to each program's revenues. Hence, $UF = R_1, R_2, \cdots, R_n$, or $U\Sigma^n_{R_1}(S \cup D)$, with the firm's aggregate utility being determined by its projects' supply-and-demand positions in the various markets. An increased supply of a product should be met with increased sales; if not, then policy should be altered either to reduce output or to employ production techniques for reducing losses and maintain revenues from sales or increase them and increase profits. A decreased supply position may be due to diseconomies in production brought about by entropy in techniques, in which case management has to restructure these techniques to compensate for the diseconomies, thereby reducing production costs and either passing on these diminished costs through price reductions or maintaining the price levels and reaping greater profits, depending on the condition of competition.

An active managerial role is essential for interpreting market activity and its impact on the firm's position. In contemporary economics there exists no hard and fast rule to be applied stating in neoclassical terms that should supply increase, prices should be lowered, and where demand increases at a rate greater than supply, prices should be raised. Supply and demand are both subject to interpretation, necessary in light of current and future short-term policies. Moreover, since more than one product is involved, the redistribution of resources in light of supply-and-demand considerations must be made on the basis of such interpretation. Managerial activity must therefore influence markets and take into account the markets' influences on the firm's policy formation and decision making.

One important factor that assists decision making and policy formation is the gearing ratio as it relates to each product in question. This ratio, which presents the firm's liquidity with respect to its assets relevant to the product, breaks down product revenues into fixed and variable costs; it thus identifies the extent of managerial efficiency relating to the product's market position and management's handling of the product in competition. When computed and analyzed, the gearing ratio indicates the firm's strengths and weaknesses as reflected in the amount of liquidity, that is, unapplied money that is, to a large extent, derived from revenues (not mustered from external investors) after costs are deducted. This liquidity provides maneuverability for further production expansion or for innovation or imitation, whichever is decided upon by the managerial board. On the basis of the gearing ratio managers have the ability to float bonds and offer shares at competitive interest rates and also provides—should this ratio be substantial—leverage on managerial staffs in other, perhaps competing, firms: either to sell out or be absorbed into the bidding firm's organization. This is done by using liquidity for acquiring substantial portions of stock and hence voters' rights, thereby being in a position to offer other shareholders better terms for their votes of confidence. This, together with the strategy of increasing efficiency to weaken the competitive positions of the target firms, making them more susceptable to takeover.

As Marris argued, the gearing ratio is subject to managerial manipulation in accordance with the objectives involved. Therefore, as well as being a sound indicator of the firm's profit and liquidity positions, any manipulated upward or downward indicates activity within the firm. By intentionally increasing this ratio and thereby increasing liquidity, managers signal that further production is being considered—production that will most likely be innovative or imitative. Although such a strategy may also mean that existing production is being expanded, this is not usually the case, for such expansion is most always conducted through the liquidity gained from the product's revenues. Directing further liquidity from other sources toward this expansion is a sign that the expected product performance has not been reached, making it doubtful that good money should be placed in the product. In all cases the manipulation of the gearing ratio depends on the ratio's utility with respect to managerial considerations. Left static, the ratio provides an accurate indication of the firm's positions of assets and liquidity; manipulated, it indicates movement in managerial strategy that is a good measurement for production.

The gearing ratio's liquidity component is the net money supply that exists after costs—such as employment, running expenses, and taxes—are deducted. Thus, $MF = L_F(Y)$; that is, the firm's available money is a function of the liquidity component of its income. Since income is derived from revenues, on the basis of its liquidity position the firm is able to attract investors should there be a large liquidity ratio to assets, allowing for a further but temporary increase in liquidity. Investors are attracted because the high liquidity is a guarantee of repayment at favorable terms; a low liquidity ratio indicates little room for maneuvering with the gearing ratio, thereby showing a high risk and a low utility rating for the firm's ability to achieve sales and casting doubts about management's ability to derive adequate profits from projects. A high-liquidity component in the gearing ratio provides confidence in management and so indicates utility for investors. Management is able to manipulate the gearing ratio, but only so far; a high ratio allows for a higher ratio by upward manipulation, but investors will consider management's presentation as an open information system and examine its performance before placing their money. If the gearing ratio appears too unrealistic, the manipulation will lose its utility and the result may be a lack of serious investors, thus affecting the offered interest rate and the ability to muster further liquidity.

Thus, the managerial role is twofold. First, management must undertake programs that will ensure the firm's position as a viable competitor for consumer demand, thereby ensuring a sufficient liquidity component derived from revenues to allow for undertaking projects of innovation and imitation. Second, management must provide a sound investment portfolio based on the firm's assets as determined by its book value, its present and potential utility, and its current production and proposed projects, providing that this information does not affect market strategy. These obligations and the ability to conduct them depend on the firm's supply-and-demand positions, which are based ultimately on internal and external market utilities.

The picture presented here has been a static one; before the firm can be placed in a dynamic setting, the equations stated thus far in this chapter should be restated:

(1) $F_t = (S \cup D)$, to which the time subscript can be added to the supply-and-demand union.
(2) $UF = R_1, R_2, \cdots, R_n$, or $U \, {}^{n}_{R_1}$ $(S \cup D-$, where UF is the firm's utility, R the total revenue, and the summation sign the total utility of the firm's operations for existing projects.
(3) $MF = L_F(Y)$, that the firm's available money is a function of the liquidity component of its income as expressed by the gearing ratio.

From these equations, it can be seen that all initiative and effort are geared for increasing demand and expanding the supply of the firm's output. These are utility-oriented equations directed to exploiting consumer demand more efficiently so that by achieving high profits, the liquidity component of the gearing ratio can be increased. This liquidity and the liquidity derived from investments strengthen the gearing ratio by providing greater freedom of action for phasing out nonprofitable projects or projects that, given managerial considerations, are no longer high priority and have therefore declined in utility. This freedom of action allows for expansion into new markets and competition in markets pioneered by other firms and promising high profits. This is the manner of the firm's dynamics discussed next.

THE FIRM AND ITS MARKETS: THE HEURISTIC LAW OF MARKETS

By quantifying the values of the equations stated in the preceding section for time t, the firm's position with respect to its markets can be stated accurately. Moreover, by quantifying the position with respect to $t - 1$ as well, the firm's comparative status can be analyzed in accordance with its past, thus forming a basis for dynamics. The firm's position in $t - 1$ gives rise to the decisions taken, the dynamics of which brings the firm to its status in t. The periods of time change as the firm's position particularly with respect to innovation and imitation changes, with regard to phasing out production lines or reducing them significantly. These decisions are taken for reasons of profit, with the implication of releasing resources and labor for programs already established or under consideration. The initiating of projects for innovation and imitation as well as reducing and phasing out existing projects are conducted for acquiring consumer demand; this activity is based on the profit motive. The detailing of these projects, the gathering of consumer data on potential consumption, and the analysis of these data are part of the managerial decision-making process on which the directions for managerial activity are formulated.

In Chapter 4 Charnes and Cooper's description of managerial activity was mentioned. You will recall their points as these: First is the planning phase, which involves the consideration of possible alternatives, including those very processes that guarantee that all relevant procedures are indeed considered. Second is the committal of resources to the projects accepted. Third is management control to determine whether the operations conform to the production processes as planned.

Due to the complexities of technology, the diversity of actual consumer tastes, the molding of these tastes to suit the firm's planning, and the adoption of production to suit these tastes, Charnes and Cooper's list is incomplete. Management activity must be expanded to five stages. First is innovative (entrepreneurial) or imitative activity, with the possibility of management considering both, depending on the projects and the available resources. Second is the planning and consideration of the various proposals and alternatives for manufacturing the accepted product or products. Third is the commitment of resources and the analysis of the feedback that this resource allocation provides, including diverting resources from other products if necessary. Fourth is the managerial assessment of the product's internal development in production and in the economies of scale and plant utility. Fifth is the external evaluation of the product in markets it pioneers, or if imitative, in the markets in which it competes.

Each of these stages, while pertaining to a specific function of management activity, relates to the internal and the external operations of the firm. The first stage, for example, pertains primarily to the external operation because it is concerned with devising a new product or placing a competitive product in a market already pioneered. Innovation and imitation, until acted upon, remain mental exercises, the fruits of speculative imaginations. This is internal to the firm, but when projected into possible market activity it becomes external, as a potential extension of the firm's market operations.

At the second stage a direct relationship exists between the external existing markets and the ideas submitted, for in the case of imitation, the difficulty is not only with offering a competitive product at a better consumer price; there is also the problem of timing and determining the duration in which other competitive products will enter the market, reducing the profit level still further. In addition, there is the consideration of extending the product into different consumer areas through previously neglected advertising. For innovation, the difficulty consists in conducting and analyzing market research results for the product's potential profitability. Constructing a market research program that will show accurately the potential response is difficult enough, especially as this requires a built-in bias for handling consumer fickleness. Management must consider the various proposals with this bias in mind. Internally, the issue of changeover in production techniques possesses its own set of problems such as altering the firm's state of production arts, formulating new techniques, and employing new concepts for handling the accepted product's manufacture. The difficulty is compounded in seeking economies of scale involving new techniques.

The third stage requires diverting existing resources from other product lines where necessary and releasing resources from existing stocks. Assessing the feedback from programs in motion necessitates the comparison of production realities and the paper models to determine where the deficiencies exist and whether the model is inaccurate to a significant degree with respect to production realities so that alterations can be made and the corrected model used for further reference. Internal efficiencies thus achieved can be passed to the consumer as lower prices. This is important for imitation, for it provides a price advantage by increasing the firm's competitive position. For innovation this is important because it allows ease of consumer liquidity allocation, thus adding to the product's appeal.

The fourth stage is an extension of the third stage: It is the consideration of alternative approaches to the product given the feedback thus far obtained in the product's development. Hence, pilot projects are often tested on select consumer groups to establish quality response and identification possibilities. Socioeconomic variations of the product are often tested, thereby deviating from the original target group to determine the product's potential for expanded consumption. Comments made as a result of this research are analyzed and incorporated into the internal model and brought into the production process, with alterations made as necessary.

The fifth stage is undertaken on the basis of consumer response as recorded in revenues. This is an external evaluation that has a direct bearing on the firm's internal operation, for while the product is marketed, feedback and revenue checks may affect resource allocation for pending innovating and imitating programs. This, the final stage in the product's development, continues as long as consumer response and internal economies maintain its viability. Hence, the firm's internal operations and the product's external development are directly related. Cost efficiency, the quality of materials used, the product's sales attraction, and the sales abilities of the firm's representatives, as well as the skills in acquiring higher liquidity that can be passed to consumers as lower prices, depend on managerial acumen in dealing with the firm's internal functioning and external market forces–and where innovation is involved, with consumer inducement for trying new products.

While each of these stages relates to both the internal and the external operations of the firm, the first and fifth stages pertain directly to the markets while the other stages maintain efficiency in production as their prime concern. It is within the context of the first and fifth stages as they pertain to innovation and imitation that the question of a law of markets must be raised once again. This question is not a deviation from the subject of the firm, its markets, and its position within the economy; it is integral. There are two reasons why. First, Say's Law has been retained in economic theory in its various interpretations in equilibrium analysis, such as its restatement in Keynes's argument, in Marris's writing, and in the macroequilibrium position of the Harrod-Domar model. The second reason is that an equilibrium position is preferred by management and is indeed sought in terms of costing, production models, and alternative planning, so that a project is developed without overproduction or underconsumption being factors and so that supply and demand eventually become equal as an increase in one is offset by a corresponding increase in the other, keeping supply and demand in equilibrium once the product has achieved sufficient market exposure. The one exception to this is during innovation, when established consumer patterns are intended to be altered and new ones formed. Once patterns are formed, however, equilibrium in production and consumption is sought along with increases in production, which occur, for example, when the product is related to other target consumer groups, offset by a corresponding rise in consumption.

While this equilibrium position is ideal, it is certainly unrealistic. With the wide range of consumer goods from which to choose, together with a limited liquidity for marginal consumption, the firm has to compete for the funds of a population that at times shows steadfast loyalty in purchasing, at times is both fickle and inconsistent in consumption patterns, demonstrating pioneer *and* sheeplike behavior, and subjected to advertising campaigns yet often unaffected by them. It is impossible for the ideal equilibrium position to be obtained from such an aggregate consuming public.

Thus, the firm tries to form a special relationship between its products and its targeted consuming public. Marris's analysis of this relationship, bringing it to the socioeconomic level, is in the main correct. Arguing that the pioneer must be considered as such with respect to a specific product, Marris places the pioneer apart from the stimuli and the socioeconomic class pressures of his peers. He divides pioneers into primary and secondary groups, with primary groups being those individuals who maintain contact with each other, and secondary groups those whose members are in contact with at least one person who has had exposure to the product—an approach that is still sound. His analysis of sheeplike behavior—the knowing about and purchasing of the product on another's recommendation—shows the manner in which many firms rely on these socioeconomic dynamics to generate consumption. These dynamics are considered by the managerial staff where innovation is undertaken and incorporated as a factor in market research, where the product's potential is analyzed with reference to other products and target groups. Both the pioneering and the sheeplike responses are considered, with the latter providing the basis of the calculated profit rate in terms of the speed of potential imitation. Where product imitation is considered, the product must be of sufficient similarity to attract customers from competing products yet be different enough to make the product unique and provide a reason for drawing buyers. These points are considered during managerial activity, for the product's success depends ultimately on the utility of consumption it offers both actual and potential consumers.

From the five stages of managerial activity stated here, it can be seen that a strict relationship exists between production, both innovative and imitative, and consumption. Management strives for equilibrium in production so that markets can be stable and profits assured; nevertheless, consumer fickleness and the market dynamics that bear on the product's cycle induce consumers to revalue their liquidity situations. The problem with Say's Law in its various forms is that it does not take into account the realities of the product's cycle and changing consumer liquidity allocation to be considered.

These five stages of managerial activity can be restated as a heuristic law of markets in which innovation and imitation are relegated to actual and projected consumption. The law is a managerial imperative, based on the profit motive, requiring production to attempt to meet potential and actual demand which it generates through the stages of managerial activity. The law states that consumption should be related directly to production in the aggregate for the firm's total output. Hence, general managerial activity is within the domain of the heuristic law of markets, thereby relegating the product cycle to second place within the overall planning and production projects. For the firm's total operation, this law of markets is a managerial obligation and a necessary factor of managerial responsibility. The manner in which these five stages of managerial activity are executed largely determines the success or failure of the firm as a competitive and dynamic economic entity. Because consumption cannot be controlled, management's success requires obtaining as much consumer liquidity through consumption as possible.

This is the motivation behind innovation and imitation, for innovation, profits are reduced once the product becomes acceptable to its consuming public; imitation sets in so that innovative profits have to be distributed among the competitors. Internal economics have to be strengthened to maintain competition, and this strengthening continues either until sales equal output or until the targeted consumer groups reallocate their purchasing in favor of other products. For imitation, as consumers shift their purchases among the competing products, managerial activity has to be directed to obtain the greatest consumption level at the lowest profit rate per unit in order to reap aggregate high profits. Thus, management has to be aware of market forces and shifts in consumer demand to be prepared for innovative and imitative projects; they must be able to release resources for these projects or for retaining a high gearing ratio for retrenchment or perhaps for both if diversification is the aim.

A consequence of this law based on the five stages of managerial activity is that the firm should plan and produce a product with the initial objective of achieving a specific quantity of sales yielding a calculated aggregate revenue (*N*) based on costs and acceptable profits; this should be targeted for a period of time that should be flexible, according to the changing conditions. Thus, although this law of markets does not necessitate *supply* generating its own demand, and although equilibrium is impossible to achieve—by the very existence of economic dynamics—by executing the five stages management generates demand through the supply of the firm's products and makes efforts to reduce overproduction and underconsumption. This is the heuristic law of markets, and a firm's success depends on the extent to which the firm applies the five stages and this law, derived from them, in light of competition.

Real equilibrium between the firm's supply of products and the demand from consumers exists only when the market for the specific products reaches saturation. At this point no new competition enters the market because it would do so only at a loss. Each firm in the competitive market has adjusted its product supply according to the consumer demand. All deviations from this adjustment are marginal, and they are conducted at the expense of other firms whose consumers vie for the specific firm's products after it has lost consumers to other competing firms. Market saturation, however, provides no guarantee for innovative or imitative profits, and the profit margin under such conditions is stable.

Under the conditions of saturation, a firm experiences a decline in its operational utility. As consumption approximates production, there can be no increased profits unless prices are increased and such increases are realized at the expenses of sales, for other competitors will maintain their prices and hence drain off the excess demand. When this situation occurs, the management begins to consider programs for innovation and imitation in markets that prove themselves to be initially lucrative, providing that their production is geared for the transformation of technology and labor to the new processes.

Hence, a firm under the conditions of saturation is at a critical stage, requiring innovation, imitation, or both in order to improve its earning position.When the gearing ratio provides sufficient liquidity, the manager's decision to act on an innovative or imitative project in accordance with the five stages of managerial activity and the law of markets derived from them will yield results after a minimum demand level achieves more than the break-even point in revenues. This requires planning and marketing, with advertising directed toward the targeted groups, at time t.

The product enters the market so that the firm's operation is now at t_1 and the supply-and-demand relationship is being formed. At this time revenues are sufficient to meet the projected results. If innovation is undertaken, revenues N will reach a basic level, increasing in time t_3 until they are reduced by imitative competition. If the product is imitative, it will occupy its position in competition, draining from other products sufficient revenues until further competition reduces the profits. This will be the case until market saturation prevents further products from competing; and although marginal competitors will drop out, the profits of each competing firm will remain fairly stable.

This product is just one in the firm's production line. The firm will undertake other innovative and imitative projects until its liquidity position is weakened through the commitment of resources and the inability to accumulate additional liquidity through transactions on the finance markets. This is a situation that confronts the firm as an individual unit in the macro economy and is the consequence of aggregate saturation and the commitment of consumer liquidity, resulting in investors' preferring the utility of liquidity to that of high returns offered for their money. At this point the economy enters a recession or depression, depending on the firms' strength of demand for liquidity and the investors' reluctance to part with liquidity. This is discussed in the next chapter, in light of our current economic situation.

THE HEURISTIC LAW OF MARKETS: FURTHER COMMENTS

A scientific law is valid as long as the conditions for which it is proposed continue to exist. However, these conditions may be altered because of changes in the field for which the law was formulated or because practitioners influence these conditions in a manner that reduces their significance, in each case rendering the law irrelevant because the conditions are no longer significant or pertinent. Whether economics is a science is not at question here, for this present writer agrees with those who profess that economics is the science of the allocation of scarce resources among competing ends for the betterment of society.

For the econometrician who accepts economics as a science, Say's Law remains problematic. Nonetheless, perhaps in spite of the difficulties it poses, it remains very active in the lexicon of economics. Indeed, theories such as those of Harrod and Domar, Marris, and Schumpeter, who sought to interpret economic activity in terms of equilibrium, have employed a version of Say's Law. The quest for stable economic activity without the uncertainty of the cycle is the very reason for the law's longevity. However, this quest must be abandoned, for in contemporary economic activity the cycle is very much in motion, rendering periods of stability—brief as they are—as special conditions in the dynamics of economic activity. Indeed, in the real world of economics Say's Law of Markets has no validity.

Say stated his Law of Markets when the Industrial Revolution was under way. The equilibrium defined by Smith as the regulating "invisible hand" was not really short-run equilibrium, but the markets adjusting its activities until its original position is reached again; yet, this equilibrium approach was made more rigorous by Say as he sought for his Law the status of science by rendering both sides of economic activity—production and consumption—as an identity that holds over time. Say based the validity of his law on his definition of the entrepreneur as one who enters a market, musters resources for production, and pays his laborers their wages, part of which they save and part of which they spend on the very goods and services produced. The savings are loaned for financing further activity, so bringing into the work force additional labor to account for increased production allowed by the investments. The workers consume the goods and services produced, so that *in toto*, consumption is generated by production. As Say's Law operates, however, consumption is regulated by production so that as a result there can be no market saturation and no cyclical fluctuations.

Reality clashed with theory but as economics is a recent science, the Law of Markets prevailed in adversity. It was Schumpeter who gave the law a unique interpretation by injecting the element of innovation into Say's concept of entrepreneurship. Indeed, according to Schumpeter, the entrepreneur is the economic innovator, living by his wits and ability to conceive new and commercially viable products. Thus, Schumpeter introduced into the concept of entrepreneurship and the economy the business cycle, and unlike Say he made the entrepreneur responsible for the fluctuations. The impact of the entrepreneur's innovation in this sense is that it brings in its wake imitators who must have sufficient capital to enter the market. Thus, as Say paid little attention to market fluctuations in the context of the Industrial Revolution, Schumpeter had much to say about them.

> Two things may be meant by periodicity [that is, fluctuations]. First, the mere fact that every boom is followed by a depression, every depression by a boom. . . . Or secondly, the actual length of the cycle may be meant. But this no theory can explain numerically because it obviously depends on concrete data from the individual case. Yet my theory gives a general answer: the boom ends and the depression begins after the passage of time which must elapse before the products of the new enterprises can appear on the market. And a new boom succeeds the depression when the process of the resorption of the innovations is ended.[3]

Innovation brings about a rejuvenation of the economy by providing competition through imitation; this brings about a Say-like condition of stability, with consumption equaling production and markets becoming saturated. This process eventually slows down when imitators saturate the market to the extent that profits drop to the point that production declines for most firms and unemployment increases as firms lay off workers to maintain a feasible profit level. Unemployment reduces consumption and the entire market enters a period of depression until the entrepreneurs disrupt the economic flow once again and revitalize the economy through innovation and bring in their wake imitators following the successful and profitable enterprises.

This interpretation may well have had a degree of validity for the period in which Schumpeter wrote, but, in retrospect, the theory was brought into sharp relief on the background of the Great Depression. The innovation that occurred then was not sufficient to revitalize the depressed economy. Investment sufficient to finance retooling could not be obtained because private investment was not really forthcoming in that climate of uncertainty. The realization that this private investment would not be forthcoming provided the basis for Keynes's argument that the government must be the underwriter for the socioeconomic social fabric. Thus, investment sponsored by government agencies would place liquidity at the disposal of consumers and translate potential to effective demand. Through sales of existing stock inventories would be cleared; through retooling, inventories would be replaced; and as a result economic activity would be regenerated.

The economic revolution of managerial capitalism that followed World War II was due to three main factors. First, there was the economic organization essential during the war years for producing a combination of war implements and consumer goods. Second, this organization required a new managerial approach for the efficient allocation of resources among competing consumer and war goods. This required keeping production costs down and finding alternative production methods without compromising quality. Third, at the war's conclusion the notion of potential consumption took on added significance as the demand resulting from released military personnel placed great pressures on industries previously engaged in war production. The transference from military to war production to offset this unleashed demand required the managerial skills built up during the war years for reorientation to new production. These factors taken to avoid the mistakes of the aftermath of World War I, with the slow transfer to peacetime production and the unemployment of released servicemen, led to the smooth transition to peacetime production and the absorption of the servicemen into industry.

The economic consequences of this transition to managerial economics was that Keynes's theory, written for the problems of the Great Depression, was rendered obsolete, except for those aspects still relevant but dissociated from the body of Keynes's theory. Post-World War II economics stressed the managerial role in innovation and imitation and in this sense bore resemblance to Schumpeter's description.

However, three differences existed between Schumpeter's theory and postwar economics. First, Schumpeter did not emphasize the impact of big firms on the economy; his entrepreneur was a small-business innovator working within the type of economy that existed during the turn of the century and the early years of the twentieth century. Second—and a point acknowledged by Keynes—the depth of depressions had become such that there existed no built-in economic mechanism for recovery. Schumpeter described the entrepreneur as the driving force of recovery, but he did not consider the complexities of the economic infrastructures that made the impact of the single entrepreneur not only marginal but also insignificant in moving the cycle upward. These two points combine with a third: He maintained the position of the traditional equilibrium concept that renders his argument for contemporary economics irrelevant.

> A knowledge of the cyclical movement and its mechanism, which is pecular to the modern business world, allows businessmen, when the worst

> is over, to anticipate the coming boom and especially its secondary phenomena [that of new businesses]; the adaptation of many individuals and hence of many values to the new equilibrium is frequently retarded or prevented by the expectation that if they can only hold out—which is often in the interest of their creditors to facilitate—they will be able to liquidate on favorable terms in the next boom or will not find it necessary to liquidate at all—which is especially important in predominantly prosperous epochs and saves many firms not really fit to live as well as many that are, but in any case retards or prevents the attainment of a settled equilibrium position.
>
> . . . Nevertheless, an approximation to a position without development always occurs, and this, being relatively steady, may again be a starting point for the carrying out of new combinations [that is, innovations]. In this sense, therefore, we come to the conclusion that according to our theory there must always be a process of absorption between two booms, ending in a position approaching equilibrium, the bringing about of which is its function.[4]

According to Schumpeter, then, through entrepreneurial activity and imitation new products are introduced and absorbed into the general flow of economic activity and a new equilibrium position is reached in which the boom has ceased and economic activity has stabilized and then slowed. Businesspeople gather sufficient information to detect when equilibrium is reached, after which they can begin their process of innovation and subsequent imitation once they find that the absorption of goods and services from the previous boom has been sufficient to warrant entrepreneurial and imitative activity.

The contemporary economic system does not operate this way. The element of timing for innovation is certainly a very important factor, one well considered before managerial approval for projects is given. But timing per se is determined by credit, consumer susceptibility toward new products, general liquidity as it influences the firm's ability to accumulate investments, and projected liquidity of the specific target and potential secondary groups. No automatism brings the economy into equilibrium so that innovation and imitation can be conducted. The opportunity for innovation depends on the firm's ability to stimulate consumption at a profitable level, regardless of the general economic condition; imitation is successful when it follows a profitable innovation and reaps profits at a level acceptable to management that considers its investment a diversion of resources. Equilibrium is nonexistent when firms close down nonprofitable operations while others begin manufacturing and distributing—each procedure with its own impact on the availability of resources, price levels, and consumer choices. Hence, the economy remains in motion. Of course, the question is, how much motion is there? And to what extent does this movement influence the general economic situation? Our contemporary condition of high inflation and little economic movement is a symptom of the serious diseconomies brought about by the business community's uncertainty and lack of confidence in the economic policies of the political leadership.

This uncertainty has an effect on the operation of the heuristic law of markets because with uncertainty comes unemployment and the consequent reduction in general liquidity. Thus, target and potential secondary groups for innovation are narrowed and imitation is thereby reduced, aggravating still further the overall economic situation. Increasingly strong competition among the innovative and imitative firms for consumers' dwindling liquidity influences the price and profit levels necessary for maintaining production and competition at a profit. The real business downturn increases so much that managers increase prices to meet and maintain a minimally acceptable profit level. The result is little economic motion and high prices accompanying the near-stagnation.

Schumpeter maintained that all inventories must be sold, "for they will indeed be produced with reference to empirically known market possibilities,"[5] and he thus invokes Say's Law once again. This does not hold for the contemporary manager—the modern entrepreneur—who innovates and imitates and seeks to match the market demand to the supply of his products. Even during the low point of the cyclical downswing, entrepreneurial activity continues with the intention of altering consumer spending patterns to realize profits. The contemporary entrepreneur not only relies on his understanding of current market possibilities but also on his ability to alter his production methods technically to reduce costs and manipulate the markets to increase sales.

The contemporary manager is a rebel, but not in Schumpeter's sense of bearing all the burden of his innovation and receiving a short-run windfall profit should his product be commercially successful. The manager is backed by the research and productive facilities of his firm and is a rebel only when he seeks to alter consumer patterns by bringing a new product on the market, directed to his specific target groups, with secondary group response anticipated. There is no equilibrium, for his innovative and imitative programs work to shift market conditions and exploit consumer liquidity.

The schemata presented in this chapter contains a supply-and-demand relationship bounded by a time-signature that changes as each decision for innovation and imitation, as well as for phasing out of products, is enacted. Revenues also change as a result of these decisions; the gearing ratio alters the liquidity component for financing new projects thus enabling innovation and imitation to change the supply-and-demand relationships for the firm's products. There is the problem of encroachment as the firm vies for the consumers of competitive products and the firm innovates and imitates partly as a response to this encroachment, with the phasing out of low-revenue products, which releases liquidity and resources for other undertakings. With management operating according to the five stages, and consequently according to the heuristic law of markets, the firm is in a state of dynamic disequilibrium, planning and executing projects, phasing out low-revenue products, and seeking to establish new markets, so that supply and demand can be matched and high profits obtained.

According to the problems of near-stagnation, high unemployment, and inflation, the firm must be placed in the context of the general economy with the government acting as a regulator before proposals can be put forward to ease the current crisis. This is the subject of the chapters to follow.

PART III
A UNIFYING APPROACH

7

INTRODUCTORY COMMENTS ON THE CYCLE

ON THE TERM *CYCLE*

The term *trade cycle*, or *business cycle* as it is alternatively called, has most certainly become a part of contemporary vocabulary. The word *cycle* is derived from the Latin *cyclus*, which is based on the Greek *kyklos*, meaning a ring or circle. The image the term conveys is that the beginning gives rise to the ending and the ending brings about the beginning. This reasoning is certainly intended in the word's usage in economics. In the neoclassical sense recovery reaches a point of overheating and results in unemployment and reduced production that leads to recession and eventually depression, with most of the productive stock lying idle. The momentum does not allow for the depression to remain but swings the cycle upward, bringing about prosperity and full employment once again.

This cycle works in the following manner. Recession sets in when the economy passes its peak of expansion, with industries reducing their supplies of inventories. Since all further expansion is nonprofitable because sales will not be made, the reduced production allows current inventories to be moved. Unemployment eventually sets in because businesses cannot maintain their employment levels. Reduced employment results in reduced aggregate sales because the work force has less money for purchases. This downward trend continues until current inventories are sufficiently depleted and the economy, declining to its lowest level, reaches depression. Unemployment has reached its peak, and since consumer liquidity is marginal, sales have declined and inventories are at a low level. Managers realize that to maintain an acceptable profit level they must increase sales. They begin reordering inventories, and this stimulates reemployment. This process continues until stocks of goods and services are fully replenished and sales increase. The downward swing, leading to depression, carries its own momentum and moves upward along the path of recovery. The aggregate liquidity level is increased; this is translated into demand. As stocks are depleted, this process continues and the movement of recovery is at a pace commensurate with the impact of aggregate demand.

The final stage in this four-part cycle is prosperity, in which the momentum of recovery expressed by the high level of aggregate demand begins slowing down. During prosperity there is near-full employment and a rapid turnover of inventories, which in anticipation of further sales begin to be replenished more quickly than they can be sold. This brings about a greater abundance of goods and services than can be absorbed by demand. The result is a marginal decline in orders, which leads to unemployment and reduction in demand. The cycle has moved from its highest upward position and begins its downward motion into recession and depression.

The neoclassical cycle is repetitive and contains elements of the two competing interpretations of overproduction and underconsumption, which stand in contradiction to the strict requirements of equilibrium. The argument that equilibrium exists in the long run as the cycle moves around a fixed equilibrium point does not hold, for according to equilibrium all disturbances in business activity are minor and are corrected by monetary and fiscal policies. Equilibrium demands stability without peaks and troughs of cyclical movement, so that explaining equilibrium within the framework of movement around a cyclical fixed point is invalid and also unhelpful.

Moreover, the neoclassical cycle has the economy on approximately the same plane of development. Contrary to this interpretation, the neo-Keynesians have been concerned with shifts in the levels of business activity and the movements that bring the cycle not to its original starting position, but to a higher plane. This means that in the course of the cycle, greater infrastructure and more production potential have been established; thus, when recovery sets in, its effects will be wider and more people will benefit. This requires higher levels of technology and therefore a trade-off between the work force and technology which leads to shifting social patterns.

Because the cycle has been considered a permanent fact of economic life, various proposals have been put forward to ease the disruptions and diseconomies brought about by the recession and depression stages. Keynes, for example, maintained that interest rates at levels required by the market forces would ease the slump and prolong the period of prosperity. In his own words:

> Thus the remedy for a boom is not a higher rate of interest but a lower rate of interest! For that may enable the so-called boom to last. The right remedy for the trade cycle is not to be found in abolishing booms and thus keeping us permanently in a semi-slump; but in abolishing slumps and thus keeping us permanently in a quasi-boom.[1]

Consider the implications of this: If market forces require higher interest rates to reduce borrowing and thus deflate the economy by reducing the money supply, but following Keynes's advice the authorities maintain artificially low interest rates through banking operations and increasing the money supply, productivity will most certainly increase but at a rate slower than aggregate demand. This will bring about aggregate price rises, with demand increasing more than supply and with prices rising continuously to offset the demand. This is a highly inflationary state of affairs resulting in upward-spiraling prices and costs with little incentive to increase supply. The quasi-boom this policy sets out to maintain will result in inflationary chaos eliminated or eased only with the economic authorities acting swiftly in the opposite direction; thus, the diseconomies for an industrialized country would certainly be great.

Another approach is that of taxation. The government levels high taxes as the cycle moves to the peak of prosperity and reduces these taxes as well as provides other monetary incentives, such as regulating the interest rates, as the economy moves to the position of deep recession and toward depression. The reasoning is that if the upswing is blunted before it reaches its peak, the downturn will not be severe. However, no guarantee assures that the blunted upward motion will lead to an easier downswing. The possibility exists that the effects of higher taxation will induce the cycle to move downward more swiftly, with resulting pullout of invested monies at a loss due to the breaking of the terms of investing. The consequence of this is postponement of projects and unemployment resulting from the decline in industrial liquidity and the uncertainty of the economic situation. This can lead to a weakened industrial and labor base, perhaps at the expense of strengthening the government bureaucracy, as answers to the economic situation are sought.

Nor is there a void of doctrinal remedies to the problems of the business cycle. A free-market economy, one in which government regulations are suffered as necessary evils, will overcome the difficulties, it is argued by those unsympathetic to labor unions, when the economic power groups act with restraint during periods of excessive prosperity with the cycle showing signs of moving higher at a slower rate. According to this argument, the government should provide the legal basis for economic activity, exerting its influence over monetary policies and interregional (interstate) affairs, and no more. A relatively unrestricted economy acts and functions well, according to this doctrine, when its participants behave in their own best interests; so when they realize that during certain phases of the cycle's movement specific modes of behavior are in their own best interests, these behavioral patterns will provide momentum to the cycle and carry it along its path.

The problem with this argument is that in spite of its doctrinaire appeal, it bears no relation to reality. For instance, at the time of the Great Depression the economies of the industrialized societies were integrated internally and externally to the point that no cyclical momentum existed to lift the economies to the movement of recovery. The "bottom dropped out," and there existed no mechanism built into the system to get things going again. Moreover, with the advent of post-World War II managerial capitalism and the dislocation of laborers by machines, the policies accepted for the Great Depression are invalid, which is one reason why the current recession is difficult to reverse: The tools are inadequate for the job.

The argument for more intervention into economic affairs is just as doctrinaire. People acting in their own best interests are not able to influence the complex areas of economics not within their immediate spheres of activity and influence. The economy is, however, under government jurisdiction in the legal sense; hence, people are subject to controls imposed on them even when those engaged in economic activity cannot comprehend the need for these controls. Indeed, controls should be exerted to move people from acting in their own best interests entirely to making their interests those of the economy in general so that the difficulties of the cycle and other diseconomies can be either reduced to the level of insignificance or eliminated entirely.

The problem of controls is that although government officials have plans for maintaining the economy, the controls they impose to direct economic activity often have unexpected results. The economy is not a mechanism but an open-ended system of information and ramifications that cannot be expected to yield desired results. If controls have any role in contemporary economics, they should be guidelines for behavior and not strict legal dictates. The contemporary economy is too complex to be so rigidly regulated; moreover, the "wisdom" of those who impose restrictions and limitations may not be so perfect nor their motives free from self-interest.

Furthermore, history bears witness to many situations in which the lack of controls leads to complete chaos, in which a passive government in times of crises leads to cynicism, distrust, and economic and social breakdown; but history also bears witness to the contrary. Economic regulations that are too extensive lead to vested economic interests becoming involved with the political authorities which in this situation provides a serious threat to the social fabric on which the economy is based, expands, and grows. Too extensive controls show that apart from the political doctrines, there is little real difference between fascist governments with the means of industry and economic development in their control and the socialist governments that control the industries and economic means under their jurisdictions.[2]

In spite of all attempts to eliminate its extreme peaks and troughs, the business cycle still remains a part of the economic system. The cycle persists over the extreme socioeconomic changes that have transpired during the development of the capitalist countries; it exists and functions in spite of the experiments to eliminate it in the agricultural, financial, and production sectors. The cycle's intensity and duration is beyond prediction, and each cycle relates to the existing conditions, or those being formed, that are unique to the particular economy in question. In a report given to the Bureau of Economic Research, Arthur F. Burns stated that

> men who wish to serve democracy faithfully must recognize that the roots of business cycles go deep in our economic organization, that the ability of government to control depressions adequately is not yet assured, that our power of forecasting is limited and that true foresight requires policies for coping with numerous contingencies.[3]

Those words were stated in 1947, when the economies of the industrialized world were moving upward from the postwar situation and the capitalist democracies were optimistic about the future. The current economic crisis shows how well these words ring true today. Those who hold the reins of governmental and industrial power have progressed little when coping with the fluctuations of the business cycle; it is deeply rooted in our economies and must be handled appropriately when crisis proportions are reached.

A DIFFERENT APPROACH TO THE CYCLE

While the trade cycle seems a permanent fixture in capitalist economies, the contemporary cycle differs from the neoclassical cycle in a significant way. The present economic crisis of near-stagnation and high inflation are unique to economies that have achieved high degrees of integration and strong infrastructures, so that all sectors are influenced in similar ways during the cycle's movement.

Because these conditions are unique to contemporary economies, the cycle must be viewed in a manner suitable to our times. Therefore, what is required is a different approach to the cycle, not within the terms of reference of the four-phased neoclassical cycle, but as three-phased cycle with the fourth traditional phase of depression eliminated. The fact is that since World War II there has been no depression with extensive idle labor and capital. This does not necessitate the presence of severe recessions such as that which we are now experiencing. Government and industrial authorities will not allow the stoppage of economic activity to the extent similar to that of the Great Depression. The argument as to whether the issue is semantic, whether high unemployment rates and low net national product is a sign of depression or recession, depends on more than a comparison of eras. What must also be considered is the composure of the economy then—its state of integration, the extent of its managerial and labor output—and the current situation, which has a substantial trade-off between the work force and automation, a highly sophisticated managerial class, worldwide markets in the case of the multinationals, and well-integrated international markets. The definition of depression for contemporary economic conditions must therefore differ from that for the past era, and this difference shows that depressions are no longer acceptable and allowable by those who exert control over the governmental and industrial aspects of the economies.

This does not mean that although the cycle will no longer drop to the depression phase, its upward motion will be more rapid and expansive. Nor does it mean that because its bottom phase has been eliminated, the momentum for its upswing will be dampened. The manner in which the period of recovery is undertaken depends solely on the vitality with which managers and government officials respond to the problems. The areas of activity are therefore political and economically innovative. It is the case that near-stagnation, pictured by the expression *stagflation*, in which inflation is high relative to output, is that imitation is still being undertaken in this time of uncertainty, in which firms with available resources enter those markets where profits can still be made, while other firms unable to undertake imitation remain somewhat dormant at the expense of their employees and resource utilization. Unemployment results and business activity slows down; to retain profits, prices are raised and costs reduced.

The consequences are welfare programs, unemployment insurance, government contracts for socioeconomic projects, and instruments for regulating the money supply and to some extent the interest rates. These measures for easing the cycle's downward swing are insufficient, however, unless industry participates actively as well. Innovation is a response to liquidity so when aggregate liquidity is low, the first effect is correspondingly and considerably slowed innovation. The secondary effect is that imitation also declines but at a rate slower than innovation because the markets have already been pioneered and have proven themselves. Near-stagnation sets in when the price rises to compensate for declining sales reach such levels that aggregate consumer liquidity has been reduced sufficiently to restrict to a great extent changes in purchasing patterns established during the cycle's movement.

The government's measures mentioned earlier maintain only a marginal liquidity, part of which is absorbed by consumption, with the remainder for savings. The accepted post-Keynesian policy of the government underwriting the economy to provide a basis for preventing the low point in the cycle's movement from being reached is itself insufficient. Industry must be brought into the economy as an active participant through innovation and imitation. Should industry remain passive—or be encouraged to stay passive—the threat to society is evident, for the influence of the government will be overwhelming, with the danger of dictatorship most certainly real. The problem is, how can government and industry act to move the cycle upward, thereby easing the crisis? This question is discussed in the next chapter.

FURTHER COMMENTS ON UTILITY

At the beginning of his discussion on the trade cycle, Keynes argued that the essential character of the cycle, and especially the regularity of both the time sequence and duration of the periods, that justifies the use of the term *cycle* is due mainly to the way the marginal efficiency of capital fluctuates. "The Trade Cycle is best regarded, I think, as being occasioned by a cyclical change in the marginal efficiency of capital though complicated and often aggravated by associated changes in the other significant short-period variables of the economic system."[4] Yet, as shown earlier in this book, the MEC is a concept easily brought into a paradox because it is based on subjective expectation that may or may not correspond to reality at the specific time under consideration.

Therefore, it is posited here that the emphasis should be placed on utility, not on the MEC. Objective utility plays the significant role in cyclical fluctuations, although subjective utility is also important in the decision-making process. It is only when the subjective aspect is transformed into objectivity through action that it makes an impact on the economy.

By shifting the emphasis from the MEC to utility, the impact of decision making comes into its own. The MEC refers to the schedule of the efficiency of capital and involves the interest rate and the trade-off between liquidity and investments. Interest rates and the liquidity-investment trade-off are important, for investments are made on the basis of liquidity and the interest rates set with respect to the liquidity on the firm's side and the willingness to hold investments over utility on the investor's side, which depends on the investor's particular subjective utility schedule, which may or may not be influenced by the firm's proposals.

It is on the basis of the firm's liquidity position and the utility schedules of its consumers that products for innovation and imitation are first considered, as this provides the profit motivation for financing further products. These considerations allow for projected utility for the products with respect to inducing potential consumers to alter their purchasing patterns and to trade off their individual liquidities for the projected products. It also induces comprehensive utility considerations concerning the firm's current production methods and analysis of potential technology with respect to future undertakings. The successful decisions taken in the previous period, moreover, determine the firm's current liquidity position and hence its potential gearing ratio, allowing managerial manipulation when necessary.

From this argument it can be deduced that there exists an aggregate utility schedule for the entire economy. This aggregate utility schedule is a macro schedule determined by the utility schedules of the industries and their individual firms, as well as by those of consumers as expressed by their preferences in purchasing. This schedule shows movement of money and resources in accordance with the various innovative and imitative programs and portrays the economy's preference for holding liquidity or investing and consuming. When the aggregate utility schedule declines to a level where liquidity as contrasted with consumption is so low that investments decline, then innovation and imitation have reached the levels of their peaks in the previous cycle. This is the turning point to recession, when the consequences of near-stagnation are approached and high inflation reached. Indeed, this is the situation we are now experiencing, and it is a consequence of managerial economics.

8

THE TRADE CYCLE IN MOTION: ON DYNAMIC DISEQUILIBRIUM

COMMENTS AND ASSUMPTIONS

The argument stated here is general because it takes into account conditions common to all contemporary managerial economies, but does not include the conditions unique to each economy. The assumption is that these economies experience similar difficulties regardless of the economic differences existing among them. Thus, there are sufficient problems uniting these economies and these problems pose the economic challenges of the coming decades.

Generally, these economies have declining net national output. Their conditions include high unemployment, low innovation but high imitation until market saturation sets in and a rapid decline sets in, and high inflation with the monetary and fiscal measures of almost no short-term avail and optimism about the future lacking. The stock exchanges reflect this situation, with prices erratic and unpredictable. Interest rates for prime borrowers are exceptionally high, pricing the medium and small borrowers out of the borrowing market. Governments are increasingly forced by the situation to abandon their traditional role of noninterference in the economy and are actively supporting those industries faced with closure and whose cessation of operations would contribute greatly to the unemployment level.

Inflation is eroding workers' savings and reducing aggregate liquidity, which is one reason for high interest rates on borrowing, since banks and other lending institutions must protect their liquidity. Businesses are becoming increasingly insolvent, with the gearing ratio reduced as a factor for accumulating liquidity. As a result, high interest rates are being charged to compensate for the uncertain future and to protect against inflation, which devalues repayment in all circumstances.

This, then, is the general domestic economic situation (the important aspect of international trade is discussed in Chapter 9). A consequence of this situation is the emergence of fringe groups and their incorporation into respectable political parties; as this is outside the scope of this present work, it is discussed briefly in Chapter 10.

The argument here is presented in its two basic components. First is discussed the micro component of the firm and its role in industry. However, the state of the economy without the influence of government places the industry in the ambiguous position of being both micro and macro: macro in the sense that the combination of industries comprises the goodly portion of economic activity and micro in the sense that it does not contain per se the influence of government policies. It is the sum total of these industries that generates economic activity, but these industries are composed of firms. Thus, the second component discussed here is government policy, with guidelines established for working to ensure dynamic disequilibrium instead of seeking to stabilize a managerial economy that by its very evolutionary position is based on disequilibrium.

Finally, further comments on the trade cycle are required. In the contemporary economic situation the image of business moving in cyclical fashion, with its peaks and troughs, is an illusion. Although periods of high and low economic activity do occur, through innovation and imitation the economy widens its base for which the corresponding infrastructure is established. When the cycle turns downward, this infrastructure remains intact, with that part which is inactive subject to reactivation when activity picks up again. The downward movement, expressed by the decline in innovation and the slower decline in imitation, does not affect the widened economic base, which is one reason that proper economic policy can eliminate the diseconomies of the sharp downswing.

Indeed, the image of the cycle moving upward and downward is inaccurate. Along with these fluctuations is the widening economic base in which the cycle moves, in which the infrastructure remains, and on which recovery and prosperity are based. The cycle must thus be viewed as moving with height, depth, and width, for this third dimension takes into account the economic expansion generated during the previous period of high innovation and imitation.

THE FIRM

As the main driving force in the economy, the firm is the basic unit of innovation and imitation and is responsible for shaping consumer buying patterns for innovative products and strengthening these patterns through imitation once the innovative responsive is shown to be positive. Thus, the firm's success depends on its managers' skills and abilities to seek out profits in new and established markets. This places the firm in a unique position of being able to generate dynamics that influence the cycle's movement and, in response, of being influenced by the cycle as it goes through its phases. This symbiotic position, as it were, must be considered by the managerial staff as it plans for short- and long-run operations.

The managers must be concerned with the product's individual cycle. This cycle differs from the business cycle in two important aspects. First, the business cycle is macro in scope, affecting the entire economy and international commerce. This cycle is recurring in indeterminate periodicity with its high and low points differing in intensity from previous cycles. The product cycle is micro as it affects the firm and the immediate market in which the product competes. The business cycle is historically repetitive. Measures taken to eliminate it in the attempt to achieve consistent growth without disturbances have proven unrealistic, and the cycle has persisted as a built-in factor of modern capitalist—and it must be added, managed—economies. The product cycle is nonrecurring. It is generated by innovation, given its peak through imitation, and fades off toward stability when market saturation is reached.

The degree to which and the rapidity with which the product cycle reaches its peak and then moves toward stability depends to a large extent on the condition of the business cycle. When the business cycle is moving toward recovery and liquidity is at the disposal of the consuming public, more innovative programs are undertaken. The emphasis is on innovation at this phase because market saturation for imitative products has been fairly complete and firms confronted with their own products' cycles will seek new markets to break from their situations and thus acquire profits. When the cycle is moving downward, whatever liquidity firms hold will be weighed for utility either to enter imitative competition or to hold the liquidity until its utility increases with respect to further production possibilities. (This is discussed further in this chapter in the section entitled "The Economy," where the relationship of the firm to the economy in the macro sense is treated.)

Consider next the firm in its micro context with regard to the cycle. Thus, consider firm F_1 during the period of prosperity. At this stage of the business cycle the firm has used its technological mix at near-maximum efficiency and has thus reached its production peak. The firm has amassed sufficient liquidity through investments and profits on sales for financing current and proposed projects and repaying loans at interest rates set at the time these loans were made.

As prosperity continues, sales are increasing, but at a decreasing rate. Signs of entropy are beginning to show, but still production is not being reduced and management is primarily concerned with expanding its imitative products through increased advertising and more competitive pricing. Sales are increasing, and although the rate of increase has slowed down somewhat, the entropy registered is not of the extent to cause alarm. Yet it is making inroads both in the production process, which is at near-full capacity, with no attempt to improve on production methods undertaken due to adequate market response, and in the external factor of near-market saturation, with innovation having ceased and management concerned with imitative programs. Management seeks imitative markets wherever a gap can be filled without requiring radicalization of the remaining productive capacity. These markets are becoming more difficult to find, and whatever idle capital there is has been more than compensated for by the large profits from the use of the productive capacity already engaged.

With the declining available imitative markets as one sign of entropy, management is confronted with another sign, that of markets that are becoming marginally profitable or beginning to incur losses. Sales slowing down in relation to production leads to stocks piling up and costly space being allocated to contain them. Attempts may be made to shift the markets to other consumer groups, but this is often not too successful, since these consumer groups at this stage of the cycle have become almost set in their purchasing patterns. This does not hold with respect to imitative products, where shifts in consumer preferences occur with great frequency, for opening new consumer markets to compensate for declining sales in the original target and secondary markets is a form of innovation with respect to consumer orientation; at this stage of the cycle consumer groups have committed their liquidity to patterns established over the cycle's movement.[1] Hence, the next step is phasing out marginal markets. The savings accrued from this reduced production increase the firm's productive capacity and—since the production line was operating at either close to costs or at a loss—also its liquidity position. Through strenuous competition, other firms impose conditions that require the phasing out of other market lines, placing the firm in a position of increasing storage costs and reduced aggregate prices for its active markets to maintain a competitive profile. Production has to decline to compensate for overall sales reductions brought about by strong competition and reduced profits from prices reduced to maintain a competitive posture. This is an inefficient use of resources, with storage space becoming increasingly scarce and productive plant forced to be idle.

During this stage of prosperity other firms also show signs of slowing down. Yet, by reducing output in markets with declining sales and by closing out those markets that no longer provide acceptable profit levels, management can maintain a fairly stable relationship with its aggregate supply-and-demand positions. The liquidity gained from closing down markets leaves leverage for considering other possibilities. Reduced labor costs, due to laying off workers as a result of market closures, together with the increased liquidity, can be either ploughed into profitable production or held for future retooling for innovation or imitation.

With the established markets reaching near-saturation, the aggregate liquidity level declines, making further imitation extremely risky, since markets for imitation have almost completely ceased to exist and innovation is unviable because of committed purchasing patterns. Investors are reluctant to continue investing because of low interest rates as the decline for money sets in, so that only special proposals that offer extremely high rates of return to compensate for the declining utility of investment money are attractive and very limited. Firm F_1 is subjected to these general market forces as it reduces its production in entropic markets. Hence F_1 is experiencing the dynamics of the cyclical downward turn as prosperity draws to an end, with market saturation setting in and a greatly reduced level of aggregate consumer and investment liquidity.

At this stage of the cycle, innovation has ceased and imitation is seriously affected. Most consumer markets are already at the level of saturation, with entry into these markets yielding at best only marginal returns. So, the mustering of liquidity and productive capital would not be worth the cost of breaking in to these markets. The exception to this would be for reducing the firm's profit-revenue ratio for tax purposes; apart from this, imitation would certainly cease being considered by the managerial staff.

At this point the cycle begins turning downward. Unemployment increases and consumption declines as salaries are replaced by unemployment benefits and welfare payments. The firm is holding liquidity because of closing marginal production lines and reducing employment accordingly. Profits on sales are reduced as consumption declines, so that managers are left with liquidity and unproductive plant. As a dynamic enterprise, the firm operates not as a function of the business cycle but within the economic opportunities the cycle provides, combining managerial skills with cost-oriented production to alter consumption patterns and establish new markets. As innovation ceases, the cycle turns downward and the firm is liquid relative to its previous position of resource committal and near-full use of productive capacity. Hence, management must either maintain the *status quo* and operate within imitative markets, thus shifting resources into those that show promise of imitative profits and closing down those that are marginal, or seek to open new markets through innovation, taking into account the risk factor of declining aggregate liquidity and committed consumer patterns. This is important in the sense that an active decision to innovate requires the accumulation of resources that are lying idle and that are available at costs lower than available during the stage of prosperity, when competition for resources drove prices upward. This also requires reemployment to stimulate marginal consumption, which may have a multiplier effect and ease the rate of the cycle's downward motion. Moreover, a successful innovative product will allow firms to enter into the new market and thus increase their employment rate rather to remain stable and liquid, as they phase out their marginal markets and opt for the liquidity position. A dynamic-oriented management can thus affect the cycle, and should this innovative process be carried to an excessive level, then the cycle's motion will be diverted and a recovery movement will begin.

The impact of such a policy on the level of aggregate prices is that it tends to lower them at first, after which they will rise and then tend toward stabilization. Lower prices result from the sellers of resources entering into new competition as they seek to move their stocks. Prices then rise as these stocks are cleared and the pressure of demand increases while supplies are reduced and as the process of restocking continues. They will stabilize as imitative products enter the markets and general consumer purchasing patterns are fairly well formed. These prices reflect the product's manufacturing costs. Through the technology of production firms seek ways of reducing these costs; but where this is not possible, they pass on or absorb the costs as initial losses to be compensated for by revenues from increasing sales.

This type of application of liquidity toward innovation makes the firm independent of the cycle and indeed may influence the cycle's motion if it is extensive enough and if other firms follow suit by innovating. However, should the managerial staff consider innovation to be of low utility at this stage and prefer holding liquidity—after computing the costs of idle productive plant and possible profits to be gained by opening new markets—then the level of the firm's output will be geared to the present and expected levels of consumption of its product range to achieve stability in accordance with the managerial law of markets. Costs are maintained and profits are also stable as consumption declines because the factors of production are made more efficient to compensate for declining sales resulting from the reduced level of aggregate utility as a function of the declining cycle.

Increasing prices, a reduced labor force, reduced output, and low aggregate utility are signs that the cycle's trough is approaching. The economic rate of growth declines as innovation ceases and imitation also stops. As supplies are reduced, higher prices are demanded for the available goods and services as the firm's managers try to maintain a profit despite declining sales. Costs are reduced as low as possible, viable products are still being produced to the levels of demand, debts on loans are being met, and investors are unwilling to depart with their liquid holdings. The cost of upkeeping idle plant increases along with the general price increases throughout the economy. Since the range of goods and services in the economy are those that resulted from the previous period of recovery, the firm's basic productive position remains unchanged, commesurate to a large extent with the previous period of recovery and prosperity, with its output consisting of the fruits of its innovative and imitative policies. The cycle has swung downward and, with the dynamics of this movement, reaches the bottom of the trough.

THE INDUSTRY

Firm F_1 is part of an industrial complex whose members are determined by common products established by imitation. The term *industry* has often been used ambiguously, sometimes referring to firms engaged in the competitive production of a single item such as automobiles, sometimes in a more general sense as the shaving-goods industry's razor blades and shaving creams. It is in the latter sense that the term is used here and to which the terms *innovation* and *imitation* relate: innovation occurs as a result of a single firm's activity within an industry in which the firm is established and in the introduction of an entirely new product or development within the given industry; imitation occurs when firms enter into competition with the production of goods and services already established by other firms within an industry. Hence, it is very common to find single firms engaged in many industries as they expand and diversify through both imitation, moving into established markets, and innovation by opening up new markets and paving the way for other firms to enter. An industry is therefore determined by the total number of firms that engage in producing its products competitively. Indeed, the productive area of the economy (and this excludes the government) is composed of the total sum of these industries and the dynamics they generate.

The dynamics of innovation and the imitation that is generated by it is one aspect of the industrial impact on the economy. Successful innovation allows the enterprising firm to gain short-term windfall profits, but these are quickly leveled by other firms entering the lucrative competition, perhaps offering better quality at lower prices because of more efficient utilization of productive facilities.

Another aspect of the dynamics of industrial development must be mentioned: This is the secondary and auxiliary industries that follow in the wake of innovation and imitation. Secondary industries are the local businesses that serve as outlets for distribution of the goods and services produced by the primary innovative and imitative firms. They include salesrooms, branch offices that may be extensions of the firms or may be independent and franchised, and local manufacturers that receive licenses to produce parts or all the products of the primary firm. Auxiliary industries are also (usually) local businesses that serve the needs of the primary firms in the local markets. These include transporters, wholesalers, and advertising agencies working with the local markets and presenting the products through the local media.

These secondary and auxiliary businesses are affected directly by the cycle's movement, often having to close down during periods of steep recession and depression and thus adding to the ranks of the unemployed. Those sufficiently strong to ride the downward motion do so at the expense of their employment levels, seeking liquidity over employment and having to adapt the levels of activity to those that correspond to their client firms. Since these are service industries, the extent of their liquidity over product can never be that great, for competition reduces profits at the best of times. The consequence is that when the cycle moves downward, the number of bankruptcies in these businesses increases; those businesses that remain achieved a sufficient numbers of clients during the periods of recovery and prosperity to be able to ride out the current difficult times.

As the cycle begins moving upward, businesses that ride out the recession are affected by the time lag between the big firms' decisions to innovate and imitate, the actual realization of these programs, and their impact on their consumer groups. The time lag is shortened considerably once these programs are in operation and the market dynamics are generated; but for innovation there is a secondary time lag between pioneering and sheeplike behavior. Granted that a large segment of the consuming public is willing to experiment with new products. But a still larger and far more significant group relies on the experimentation of others, and its convictions afterward are strengthened by the advertising and terms of sale. Firms keep in mind their effect on this larger group when they choose the most efficient secondary and auxiliary businesses for increasing appeal of their products and stimulating sales among pioneering and sheeplike consumers.

As recovery continues with more new and imitative products on the markets, the time lag between innovation and imitation varies with the allocation of consumer liquidity and the formulation of preferences based on individual utility ratings. The secondary time lag between pioneering and sheeplike behavior also varies according to the new products and consumer liquidity allocation. The duration of these time lags is very short—a response to the liquidity resulting from recovery and approaching prosperity—but no fixed economic theorem can determine with any accuracy their spans.

As the cycle moves from recovery to prosperity, innovation increases at a decreasing rate with imitation expanding according to the market opportunities. Because consumer liquidity has become committed, backlogs tend to occur in the holdings of the secondary and auxiliary industries. Discounts are offered, sales announced, and other consumer incentives proposed to keep the goods and services moving; however, this does not reduce stocks sufficiently to induce greater output by the firms, so that these businesses are left to rely on their managers' initiative and ability to use whatever tactics are required to unload these goods and services, so maintaining their businesses as viable enterprises. Inadequate policies result in bankruptcies—a consequence of riding the peak of prosperity.

Hence, the dynamics of innovation and imitation result in the growth of local businesses as means of distributing and supplying the products. As the industry's firms expand through their market operations, these businesses also expand through their handling of the goods and services. During recovery and prosperity, the big firms and local businesses enjoy the benefits; during the decline and recession of innovation and imitation, both industry and the affiliated local representatives suffer the decline in profits.

THE ECONOMY

In the last chapter it was mentioned that depressions are obsolete because governments can apply measures to prevent the complete stagnation of economic activity and the mass unemployment characteristic of recessions. Yet, in the preceding discussion it was explained that the cycle was brought down to the level of depression. This latter comment was not an attempt to explain the contemporary business cycle in terms of the neoclassical reference, which of course would be a glowing inconsistency. The business cycle illustrated in the preceding section was brought to the level of recession to highlight a difficulty in contemporary economic semantics. If recessions are to be measured against the conditions of the Great Depression, if this historical crisis is to be the bearer of the criteria for recessions, then the business cycle, no matter how low it falls, will never again reach such depths—assuming that responsible governments are in control. If, on the other hand, each situation is to be judged according to its own standards, such as the extent of economic decline with respect to the economic levels of growth achieved during recovery and the early stages of prosperity, then there is no reason to prevent the cycle's downward position, when it becomes extreme, to be considered a depression. Of course, such a definition may be repugnant in the contemporary politician's lexicon. To avoid all confusion, therefore, the depression stage will be termed a severe recession.

This definition and its abolition of the term *depression* is not to sooth the politicians' wounds but is based on sound economic reasoning. The economic infrastructure established during the previous period of recovery is substantial, and the quality and quantity of goods and services is greater than in the previous period. Combine these facts, established during the innovative and imitative periods, and compare them against the previous cycles, and the cumulative effects of economic growth are visible.

This situation contrasts to the Great Depression, where the preceding cyclic movements preceding the depression offer no basis of comparison, but where the economy collapsed almost absolutely. The cumulative effects of previous growth periods were wiped out as the banking system and industrial networks collapsed and as the stock exchange saw the elimination of many businesses and entrepreneurs. Although the present world economic crisis is severe and many people are affected, it is nothing like the Great Depression. Government bodies have learned the lesson of underwriting the economy.

Another point must be made here. To maintain that the business cycle carries its own momentum moving in its phases as a machine in perpetual motion is a neoclassical fiction based on economic determinism. How does this accusation relate to the fact that the cycle is inherent in economic activity? The given example demonstrates that the cycle need not operate in a consistent pattern. It is innovation and imitation, programs carried out within the context of each firm's abilities, that determine the firms' positions with regard to their performance. These programs, when acted upon industrially and intensively, can prevent or delay the movement of the cycle (as discussed in the example). Indeed, the business cycle is a force generated by the dynamics of closed-ended product cycles and by the managerial decisions based on liquidity positions formed through revenues from investment gains. Moreover, as these conditions are generated, they bring about dynamics unique to their circumstances, which have a significant bearing on the end-and-final-motivation, the consumer. Whatever differences of opinion exist among the managers of the firms, they share one thing in common—their profit motive. In general, these managers act rationally so as not to threaten intentionally their profit positions during periods of high innovation and imitation and when the reality is such that profit positions and loss minimization are at a trade-off.

These managerial actions are based on the utilities of the programs, both subjective and objective. Objective utility has prime importance, since this is the probabilistic interpretation of the viability of information pertaining to the programs and it is on the basis of this utility that are formulated subjective utilities, in which decision makers order their personal preferences and choose to enact certain programs and to delay the implementation of others. These actions have their effects on the economy and as the programs get under way, their dynamics are generated and incorporated into the objective utilities confronting the economic decision makers.

Given the importance of objective utility and subjective utility in the decision-making process, how do these utilities influence the business cycle and in what manner are they influenced by the cycle in turn? Basically, the cycle moves in response to the expansion and contraction of innovative and imitation, and the decisions to act on these projects, or not to act, depend on the firms' objective utility positions, the objective utility ratings of the proposed projects as best they can be determined, and the managers' subjective utility preferences for the proposed projects and their decisions to act or not to act on these projects.

The business cycle is a cumulation of product cycles and liquidity positions of the many firms and of industries that the firms compose. During the time which product cycles tend to stabilize, other projects are introduced either through innovation or imitation; because liquidity is fully committed and further new production is unfeasible, then the firms' liquidity positions become unstable as their products are subject to the rigors of competition and their sales revenues are consequently influenced downward.

In the earlier discussion about the firm (see "The Firm"), comments were made on the product cycle with respect to the general business cycle. Consider now how the cumulative effects of the product cycles of the various firms bring about the aggregate business cycle, while they influence industries and the economy *in toto*.

Consider firm F_1 in time t_n, in which it has high liquidity and its production is imitatively oriented. The dynamics of the cycle will be suppressed for the moment in order to isolate the firm as a working unit to show how it generates dynamics. Since its markets are imitative, the firm has achieved the requirement of the heuristic law of markets in which its supply and demand are fairly stable and all fluctuations that do occur are minor and require no serious managerial attention.

With stability and high liquidity, managerial decision making is oriented toward innovation. Liquidity is channeled into innovative production, and sufficient market research has yielded a high utility rating for the proposed project. Entering the market with sufficient advertising to generate pioneering consumption of the product in time t_{n+m} (*m* being the time of marketing) generates the interest of managers of other firms. As sales increase and the consuming public responds, F_1 has initiated a market that draws imitations and initiates new growth. The profit of F_1 is reduced according to the extent of competition; eventually a point of growth will be reached in F_1's product cycle where growth will decline to a level of stability, thereby reflecting once again, and for this particular product, that supply is stable with a product's demand position. The same occurs with the products of competing firms until market saturation allows for no further competitive entry.

Hence, over time, the innovative product has led to the development of a new market and economic growth increases accordingly. This, in itself, is insufficient to generate the dynamics of the aggregate cycle. The point is that as consumption is drawn toward the new product and its competitors, it is drawn *from* other sources. The money for consumption may be taken from savings, in which case the liquidity position of the institutions from which it is taken is reduced and their funds available for investments decrease. These funds may be taken from other patterns of consumption in other markets, bringing about the phasing out of those competitive firms whose profits are marginal, thereby increasing their liquidity or proclivity toward innovation, with dynamics generated through innovation.

Still, these dynamics in themselves are insufficient to generate the aggregate business cycle, for the relocation of money brings about a decline in one economic sector while raising the growth level of another. Shifts in consumption patterns are no causes of cyclical motion per se, unless these shifts are large. Innovation and imitation are effective only when they reach their target groups, and these are the so-called grass-roots consumers who allocate their liquidity according to their inspired and accumulated tastes and preferences. That innovation and imitation bring about shifts in consumer spending is not sufficient to generate cyclical movement in the economy when undertaken on a small or even moderate scale.

Therefore, although firms themselves may be affected by consumer fickleness, these changes are insufficient to generate the cycle. The cycle is generated by the cumulative effects of innovation and imitation and the establishment of consumer purchasing patterns for the duration. Again, consider the position of liquidity among the majority of the firms. This liquidity position is high due to the preference for liquidity brought about by the phasing out of products with low utility and the costs saved therefrom in the form of labor and expenditure. Fixed capital expenditures are written off in taxes so that the short-term payments are cancelled by the long-term returns on costs. The point is that a high liquidity position is the result of a decline in economic activity; this increases the gearing ratio and provides the basis for accumulating investments of a level sufficient to underwrite the innovative and imitative undertakings that management is unable or unwilling to apply to its own liquidity. In other words, this indicates that economic activity has declined to the low trough of the cycle's movement.

The accumulation of liquidity allows for the initiation of projects not previously acted upon but of sufficient market utility to be activated when market conditions are right. Production has declined generally in the economy and prices are high because consumer goods and services are in short supply compared to the earlier cyclical phase. Many firms opted for liquidity over production because their products have reached the stable stage in their cycles and revenues have been reduced because of competition. This has resulted in a scarcity sufficient to drive the prices upward. Moreover, the employment level has declined as firms seek to increase their liquidity because of revenues lost due to sales loss from ceased production. High prices together with unemployment bring about a psychological socioeconomic condition in which innovation is carried out reluctantly and consumers change their purchasing patterns mostly by restricting their consumption. To alter this economic and social climate, innovation as a trade-off against liquidity must get underway so that employment can increase and new purchasing patterns can be established. The underwriting of this psychological socioeconomic climate is the task of government (this is discussed in the next section of this chapter).

Innovation requires reemployment to move the production lines. This in turn leads to the development of local secondary and auxiliary businesses thereby increasing general employment and hence consumption liquidity on the grass-roots scale, where the actual consumption occurs. This so-called grass-roots position is, not a rigid, but a flexible socioeconomic rating of various income groups, targets for the advertisers seeking to promote the firms' goods and services. The composition of these income groups varies with the effects of each completed cycle as some people fall to a lower income group while others increase their standing. The consequences of innovative and subsequent imitative production are therefore the revival of the economy, the reemployment of workers and the increase of their purchasing power, and the shifting of consumer patterns so that those products unable to retain their utility in the reviving economy are phased out, thus giving the producers greater liquidity to enter other competitive production. The result is the ultimate widening and deepening of the economic infrastructure. Thus, with revived innovation and the following imitation, on a large scale, the cycle moves upward and recovery is underway.

This process continues until employment is full—as defined by the government—and most of the aggregate industrial capacity is utilized.

As innovation and imitation continue in its wake, purchasing patterns are established. These purchasing patterns are for products, not brand names, the demand for which fluctuates as bargains are offered and competition quality is improved. Some competitive product brands are phased out as competition takes away their sales. With employment near full capacity and imitation slowing down because the reduction of innovative products brings few new markets, the cycle continues to move upward, though at a decreasing rate. This is the period of prosperity, and it contains the dynamics of the impending downward movement.

Prosperity increases, but entropy sets in, eventually slowing down the economic dynamics and moving the cycle toward depression. Without significant innovation, imitation declines and for a while full employment provides sufficient consumer liquidity to maintain this level of growth. Competition becomes more rigorous as firms not investing in new products vie for each other's customers, phasing out products of low competitive utility and bringing about unemployment. The period of prosperity passes its peak, and the cycle turns down toward recession and if unchecked ultimately to depression.

Recession is marked by increasing numbers of unemployed, increasing bankruptcies, and inflation as prices are raised to protect profit levels and compensate for the reduced production resulting from the phasing out of low-utility goods and services. The situation worsens as inflation increases due to the decrease in aggregate liquidity for consumption brought about by rising unemployment. Innovation has all but ceased and imitation is unprofitable because those products that are phased out are not readily replaced by other potential competitors because of the decline in consumer liquidity. Recession is a dynamic process that continues until the cycle reaches its lower plateau of depression, after which a time lapse is required to move the cycle upward.

When the cycle does begin its upward motion, the economy is not of the same composure as its previous cyclical completion. It has been altered due to its product composition. Its secondary and auxiliary businesses are different and oriented toward promoting different products; the process of distribution has altered as new businesses replace those that as a result of mergers or bankruptcies no longer remain. The big firms are different in the sense that their technologies have been altered to cope with the new production and the competition that invariably ensues. Target groups have changed to cope with the different compositions of socioeconomic income groups that have formed as a result of the cycle and the consequences of recession and depression. The economic infrastructure has been broadened by the new products and the technological changes incorporated to produce them.

THE ECONOMY AND GOVERNMENT

The discussion so far has assumed the role of government is suppressed. Left on its own, the dynamics of economic growth will move the economy through the four cyclical stages, with the level of prosperity different each time, so that if illustrated graphically prosperity would be on a different set of coordinates, moving upward and to the right. Indeed, each cycle must be so represented indicating the unique growth bases for each cyclical motion.

Nevertheless, the point, made by Keynes and accepted by every macro economist ever since, that the downward swing should be minimized and the upward swing extended is certainly the goal of the government. As shown, the economy that functions without the government cannot achieve this. The cycle will fall steeply until it levels off at the depression phase, then to swing upward again. The government's role should be to operate within the economy to minimize the downward swing and extend the upward swing. The question is, how is this to be done?

In contemporary managerial economies the depression phase of the cycle is neither necessary nor wanted. It is a period of stagnation, where unemployment reaches its peak and production almost ceases, where innovation has come to an end and imitation does not function. It is a period of temporary duration in which much socioeconomic suffering exists and for which there is no economic or philosophical justification for its existence. Since the depression phase is an extension of recession, it can be stopped at the opportune moment so that the downward movement is halted.

Of course, since as each cycle has unique characteristics, the "opportune moment" must be calculated within the context of each cycle. The extent of unemployment must be gauged against the aggregate liquidity requirements necessary for the undertaking of innovative projects and against organized labor's willingness and ability to tolerate unemployment levels. The present utility of consumer purchasing power must be assessed against its potential future purchasing power as predicted by big business and organized labor in bargaining for new wage structures. Government officials must assess when to stop underwriting unemployment, given the costs for doing so as the unemployment rate increases with the cycle's downswing and given big business's costs of reemployment during the cutoff point for revitalizing the economy as determined by government officials. The socioeconomic costs of approaching stagnation and increasing inflation must be assessed against the costs of revitalizing the economy by reducing inflation and eliminating stagnation at the time considered. Therefore, the level determined sufficient for recession to have served its objective of clearing markets, eliminating redundant products through their being phased out, and generating unemployment to increase firms' liquidity ratios must carefully be assessed, analyzed, and agreed upon by big business, organized labor, and the governing officials.

It is best for these power blocs to discuss their respective views on these issues, but it is also somewhat naive to suggest that an agreement on the cutoff point and the actions to take to revitalize the economy can be reached easily. Organized labor and big business are historical and natural protagonists; government, relying on the support for big business funding for elections has not overlooked the fact that labor has also become big business in its own right, for it controls the strike weapon and largely determines the degree of consumer liquidity through wage bargaining; and it accumulates its funds through membership dues and investments.

There is, however, an important reason why such an agreement must be reached—strictly from the point of view of power-bloc self-interest. Businesses have to stand and face strong competition, and neither depressions nor steep recessions are to their advantage. As the cycle moves downward a point is reached where the trade-off between the costs of employment and maintaining liquidity is no longer to the firm's advantage. This happens when the costs of upkeep and expenses begin to reach the amount of revenues gained from sales.

Labor's interests are also served best when the cutoff point is reached because wages can be structured and employment maintained, without the increasing unemployment accompanying the cycle's recession motion. This is also to the advantage of big business, since employment maintains consumer liquidity and provides incentive (the profit motive) for innovative and imitative projects. Also, it reduces the pressure for government action to reduce unemployment and to inject money into the economy, a move which lacks industrial backing and increases consumer liquidity without the goods and services for consumption, thereby increasing inflation.

Reaching the cutoff point is also advantageous to the government, which is duly elected and which must therefore act to ease the economic crisis or face an angry electorate during election time. As mentioned, injecting money into the economy without the backing of industrial output increases consumer liquidity, which is siphoned off by inflation—in other words, this move solves nothing except keep the electorate temporarily quiet.

Traditionally, that is within the post-Keynesian era, government acts to maintain the economy in equilibrium, seeking to defuse inflation and stimulate the economy when signs of deflation threaten. Taxes and government contracts are the tools government employs to achieve the desired goal of equilibrium with growth. The consequence of applying these tools to contemporary economies can plainly be seen with the current prolonged recession, which is getting deeper in much of the world and bringing about much economic and political unrest.

This is, again, another example of trying to cure the disease with standard medicines to which the disease no longer responds. Not that these post-Keynesian tools have been used indiscriminately; rather, they have been applied in a manner that is ineffective for objectives that make them impossible to achieve. Since the firm is the generator of economic growth, it does not comply to the principle of equilibrium, no matter how strongly the heuristic law of markets is applied. There can never be equilibrium between supply and demand over the medium- and long-run periods because of the necessity to phase out certain products, to channel resources toward the development of other products, to opt for liquidity over production, and to open new markets. There are the rescheduling of production quotas due to competition and the offering of consumer incentives to increase sales—the direction of which cannot be predetermined. If economic stability exists, if the disequilibrium situation is stilled, it is when the depths of depression are reached; this is short lived because management seeks ways to stimulate production and demand once more. The heuristic law of markets is a managerial goal, an ideal to stabilize production goals; it conflicts with the reality of economic competition and consumer fickleness.

For example, the *ad hoc* policy of taxation—increasing taxes to siphon off excess purchasing power or lowering them to increase aggregate liquidity—is certainly ineffective as a policy on its own. Liquidity should be increased or reduced according to the requirements of business and not strictly from the government's point of consideration.

When recession begins to intensify, firms trade off liquidity for employment and production; to reduce their liquidity through taxation forces firms to lower prices temporarily so they can become more competitive and thus preserve their liquidity positions. This results in increased sales, which has the effect of raising prices higher than taxes to maintain liquidity without having to hire workers to increase production. Continuous tax increases in this situation result in extreme economic distortions, the inefficient application of money, and the diseconomic utilization of resources.

On the other hand, increased liquidity through tax breaks may encourage the further trading-off of production and employment for liquidity to avoid future borrowing and eliminate interest payments on loans. The option for liquidity may also be based on uncertainty over economic conditions, since imitation has become unprofitable and innovation unfeasible due to the lack of available consumer liquidity. In other words, tax reforms may allow the recessive phase to continue moving downward unimpeded.

Increasing personal liquidity by easing taxes may result in greater consumption but at higher prices, since firms are not very willing to increase their output because of having opted for liquidity. This may fan the flames of inflation still further. On the other hand, decreasing consumer liquidity through higher taxation may effect massive restrictions in purchases, restrictions for which firms are not prepared, and thus induce firms to make drastic price reductions and phase out many competitive products because of their rapid loss of profitability. Because demand is strong and supplies restricted, the result will be price rises.

Supporting industries by placing orders is usually a method of seeking to stimulate *ad hoc* production on the assumption that money injected into the economy and backed by production is viable in providing liquidity based on productivity and therefore is important in reviving a recessed economy and ensuring a degree of employment. This reasoning is founded on the multiplier effect, where the money earned is partly saved and partly directed toward consumption. The money saved is invested in industry and that part directed for consumption stimulates production—so the argument goes. This is not necessarily so, for increased production in one sector or one industry may stimulate investments that may not be directed toward financing other industrial projects, since unsuitable interest rates may preclude investors on both sides of the transaction from reaching an agreement. Moreover, production may not be stimulated to the extent of being increased sufficiently to offset price rises but may lead to further inflation if demand is stronger than supply. There are no guarantees here either, unless massive and noneconomical industrial support is allocated, in which case productivity will increase and production will be made competitive again. Such a measure, however, would require such government financing that it would not pass through the political channels to be accepted.

Regulating the interest rates is also a technique that government has employed. This measure is taken on the assumption that if rates are low, investments will be required and demanded by the firms for project financing, which will stimulate industrial output, which in turn will reduce unemployment and move the cycle upward. The difficulty with this is that low interest rates relative to the current economic conditions may encourage firms to seek investments but will not encourage investors to opt against the liquidity position. Thus, the interest rates will not remain artificially low and will rise, according to the demand for liquidity, to the level suitable to the market conditions.

The opposite effect also holds. When the government raises interest rates, it is to encourage investors to find markets for their liquidity; it does not encourage firms to seek investments. The economic conditions will therefore force the rates down to the level where managers and investors agree to enter into business transactions.

The difficulty with these programs is, not that they are ineffective per se, but that their application makes them ineffective as tools for solving the economic problems. The post-Keynesian ideal of minimizing the business cycle and maintaining the economy on an upward growth path is unattainable because of the very dynamics of innovation and imitation. New products will always appear on the market, and if successful these will be followed by close imitators. Markets will always reach near-saturation with unemployment resulting as products are phased out and firms opt for utility. The cycle in the democratic managerial economy cannot be prevented.

Nor can attempts be made by the governing authorities to minimize the recession and maximize recovery and prosperity. As the current crisis shows, however, their approaches are of little utility: They are post-Keynesian in orientation and designed for equilibrium growth, and therefore they are of no great bearing on the economy. What is required is a concerted effort by organized labor, the managerial staffs of the big firms, and government representatives to reach agreement as to how far the recessive phase of the cycle is to move downward and where the cutoff point should be.

Each cycle is unique because it is based on the conditions established by the previous cycle. There are, of course, common generalities such as unemployment, inflation, idle capital, and idle liquidity. These, however, remain abstractions until placed in the context of each specific recession to determine their composition and extent. Government measures are impositions placed on an economy over which there is no response control, which is why the consequences of these measures are not necessarily those that are sought. Regulating interest rates without discussing the perspective of those who work with these rates—how they consider the results of such manipulations and perhaps other alternatives—merely results in the consequences discussed earlier. Backing specific industries with the hope that this will result in reemployment and stimulation of the economy, without considering the consequences on the productivity of the backed firms, and that of firms that are supposed to benefit from the money injected into the economy as a result, may only increase the economic difficulties and increase inflation. Taxation manipulation has yet to prove itself a viable form of economic regulation.

How is a cutoff point to be determined and what measures can be taken to reverse the cycle? The cutoff point should be determined by assessing the extent of business's opting for liquidity rather than production, given the current conditions. From the business perspective, this must depend on consumer willingness to shift from current purchasing patterns to those that have yet to be established through marketing. In other words, the determinant must be the viability of possible innovative products given the current consumer patterns. This requirement depends on the amount of liquidity held for consumption as compared with consumer income already allocated for consumption and savings.

Labor's perspective, of course, differs, as it is to labor's disadvantage that unemployment should be other than marginal, that is, frictional and in part seasonal. As long as unemployment increases, organized labor will find itself in with disillusioned supporters who withdraw their financial backing and their votes for those whom they elected to represent them. The cutoff point for labor will therefore be at a higher level of the recessive cycle than that opted for business.

The government's cutoff point will be based on a combination of factors. First the government must consider the theoretical post-Keynesian factor of preventing all major economic disruptions, that is, all recessions, by seeking measures to keep the economy in an equlibrium growth position. Second, government must consider the position of big business, since this is the factor that provides employment and growth. Third, the government must consider the attitude of big labor, for this political bloc controls much influence with the voting public. Fourth, the government must consider how the common voter not affiliated officially with business nor labor fares in the economic recession.

The problem is, given the uniqueness of every cycle, on what basis can a cutoff point for halting the cycle's downward motion be reached, given the vested interests and common grounds for reaching an agreement? This can be determined from assessing the percentage of unemployment tolerable for organized labor (excluding frictional unemployment), the degree at which employment is preferred to nonproductive liquidity for business, and the extent to which low productivity and unemployment remain politically harmless for the government. Labor economists, government statisticians, and business economists can therefore pool their resources to place these considerations into a working formula, find the cutoff point agreeable to all concerned, and take actions appropriate to the given situation. This is surely a better way of spending money and intellectual energy than combating recessions in ways so far proven futile and of no utility. So far, the cycle has been resistant when the "cures" have been applied and has moved in its own natural way regardless of attempts to restrain it. Hence, labor, business, and government decision makers should direct their efforts to determining where the cycle should be stopped in its downward movement and which methods should be applied to achieve this end.

Of course, the question should be, which methods will not only stop and reverse the cycle's path? First, it must be clear that the joint decision makers must agree on the cutoff because if not, then all measures that are taken will be of no effect. This is because the forces still in operation will negate those forces that are introduced and override them. If there is less than full cooperation from labor, business, and government, the efforts will be futile and the cycle will ride out its path unperturbed.

What, then, are the methods to not only stop and reverse the cycle? First, when the cutoff point at which business opts for productivity over idle liquidity is reached, the governing bodies should ease consumer taxes and increase the amount of money injected into the economy. Consumer taxes should be eased to increase the money available for spending and saving. This money would not be available until the fiscal year is completed; so the injection of extra money into the economy will serve to stimulate consumption and production. These measures without the cooperation of business would lead only to greater inflation as more purchasing power competes with limited goods and services. Of course, labor's cooperation is essential here to allow for the institution of better production methods, perhaps at the short-run expense of reduced employment under the present circumstances. It is a fact of economics that where short-run unemployment results from improved production techniques, medium-run employment increases to absorb the unemployed as production increases and competition places demands on the labor market. An added benefit is that those employed at later stages of production acquire the skills that have been developed during the earlier stages and thus have the advantage over those employed earlier in that these skills are relatively free from the difficulties of the "running-in" period. Furthermore, wages should be kept in line with the economic conditions as wage earners are compensated by tax reductions and by the extra money injected into the economy to stimulate consumption.

During this period unemployment benefits must be maintained to keep a basic consumption level for those not readily compensated by becoming employed. Should the government consider investing in projects, this could be done once the dynamics of this operation begin to take effect, since this investment will be backed by the productivity it stimulates and the projects of other firms in the production and marketing stages. This injected money will be backed by aggregate output and price reductions as firms begin to compete for consumer purchasing.

Interest rates pose a problem of their own. Here, the government's influence should be marginal, acting on banks and government-backed savings and loan associations and building societies. Interest rates fluctuate according to the aggregate utility of liquidity and investment. Thus, the government should provide incentives in the form of lowering the banks' and other institutions' capital-investment ratios so that liquidity is that more easy to accumulate. Any attempt to force interest-rate mobility will lead only to distortions in the supply and demand for money and will tend to retard the benefits of the other programs.

The consequence of these methods is that they stimulate both production and consumption. Before the enactment of these methods, imitation was beginning to taper off and, except for the brave firm that ventured on the market with a new product and siphoned some of the established consumption and generated competition with its product, innovation had ceased. With production stimulated and with consumers possessing additional liquidity, the processes of innovation and imitation can begin anew and move the cycle toward recovery and prosperity.

The question remains, should measures be applied to curb prosperity or to maintain it to prevent the cycle's turning downward? The answer is that the prosperity phase should be left alone because it is increasing at a decreasing rate and so allows industrial activity to slow down. Thus, a downturn can eventually set in, allowing the markets to clear themselves as the cycle moves toward recession. Labor, business, and government decision makers can then determine another cut-off point that will allow the motion to be halted after sufficient market clearing and after managers have had enough time to consider proposed innovative projects and to plan their strategies for production, advertisement, and distribution. Consumers will have time to reconsider the utilities of their purchasing patterns and be psychologically prepared for new products; labor will become entrenched in its working patterns and entropy will set in, so that workers will be prepared for new employment possibilities when the cycle moves downward and they become unemployed. Government will be prepared to take unified steps along with business and labor to reverse the cycle, instead of relying on *ad hoc* and inefficient measures to stop and reverse the cycle. Applying these methods in a unifying manner can limit recession and extend prosperity, the objective since Keynes stated this point.

PART IV
RAMIFICATIONS OF THE UNIFYING APPROACH

9

ON INTERNATIONAL TRADE

INTRODUCTION

In 1937 Jacob Viner wrote, "The 'classical' theory of the mechanism of international trade, as developed by Hume and J. S. Mill, is still, in its general lines, the predominant theory. No strikingly different mechanism has yet been convincingly suggested."[1] In retrospect, it may seem that Professor Viner was somewhat hasty when he wrote these words, for *The General Theory* had already appeared with many of Keynes's contributions and those of his followers already incorporated into the lexicon of international economics. Such terms as the international multiplier, the marginal propensities to save and consume, the accelerator, and the MEC are now and were then linguistic and conceptual tools of the international trade economist. Moreover, as the economies of the world's nations meet in international commerce, the post-Keynesian international trade theorists are certainly justified in adapting concepts originally developed for the national economy to meet the requirements of the international arena.

Regardless of the lapse of decades since Professor Viner made this statement, considering the manifold changes in economics and its theories that have occurred since then, much of this statement's sentiment remains justified. The general theory of international economics remains relatively close to the theories Hume and Mill treated, rendering international economics the dubious honor of being the most neglected branch of economic theory.

The reason for this state of affairs is historical. It is due to the almost total rejection of mercantilism after the publication of the *Wealth of Nations*, which had the result of placing the economic focus primarily on the national economy. Indeed, the classical and neoclassical economists, in their discussions of the causes and origins of national wealth, relegated international trade to a mere extension of domestic economic activity—a position that is clearly false.

Mercantilism was strictly a British approach to economic wealth and differed radically and indeed contrasted with its French counterpart of physiocracy. In the cool rationalism for which French thought is traditionally famous, Physiocracy was a philosophical-cum-economic theory which maintains that a country's wealth stems from its soil. Agriculture was the most important industry, for it provided the food necessary for feeding the population. On the basis of surplus foodstuffs, trade would enable these foodstuffs to be exported for goods and services not obtainable domestically, thereby increasing the nation's wealth. The greater the crop's yield, the hardier the livestock yields and the stronger the economic position.

The mercantilist school differed from and rejected the logical physiocracy of the French. In the tradition of empiricism and experimentation, the British maintained that a nation's wealth is based solely on its trading prowess. It was of no significance whether the goods traded were domestic or acquired from other lands. Wealth was proclaimed in coin obtained by trading more than was recevied in goods and services with the surplus made up in coin, thus having a claim on the other's economy. All surpluses in the trade balance were dealt with in this manner, and trade was sought primarily to obtain foreign coin.

The difference in the British and French approaches to trade are also noticeable in their approaches to exploration. They both engaged in conquest for the expansion of their power, encouraging sailing and conquering. The British, being an "island country," were aware of the burden of markets placed on them by the geographical separation. Although they did not neglect the agricultural sector, they did recognize their limited space and lack of resources; they thus sought resources and cheap labor to direct their activities to trading to obtain foreign coin.

The French approach to exploration was to conquer new agricultural lands so that their produce could be traded under French rule, thereby increasing the goods and services to be obtained for their markets. They enslaved conquered peoples to till the soil and increase agricultural yields, while the British employed slave labor in both agriculture and in the manufacturing process, as it existed then, to increase output for foreign trade.

These two different philosophical and realistic approaches found common ground in the reasoning of Adam Smith. His French was sufficient to allow him to engage in deep philosophical discussions with Dr. Quesnay, the main spokesman for the Physiocratic school, and he debated Dr. Quesnay's followers. The results of these arguments are found in Smith's great treatise.

Smith recognized that the degree and kinds of enterprise existing in Britain and France were not adequate for economic expansion. Guilds and other forms of unions which protected the status of their members and the qualities of their trades were preventing economic growth. Instead, private free enterprise should be undertaken in which individuals take the risks and reap the profits. While Smith considered agriculture to be of prime importance, he deflated its physiocratic significance and placed it soundly in the economic function of feeding the populace. Surplus agricultural produce could most certainly be exported and goods not produced in the local economy imported. International commerce should not be neglected, as this is important for stimulating production and earning foreign coin. Emphasis should be placed on individual initiative and enterprise as the means of building the wealth of nations because enterprise brings into the markets new products and creates demand. Therefore, both agriculture and exporting should be consequences and supportive economic factors of private enterprise.

Historically, the impact of the *Wealth of Nations* is that it pointed inward to the development of national economy based on individual initiative and enterprise. This was of such importance that the readers of Smith's work paid little or no attention to his contributions to international trade. The focus was internal, on the division of labor and entrepreneurship as the factors of economic growth and development.

These were the arguments taken up by Say, Ricardo, Malthus, and the other classical economists. Smith's followers took up various aspects of his reasoning. Malthus emphasized the significance of agriculture and cast a warning over industrializing nations that population growth would outstrip the growth of food supplies with the result of famine, disease, and premature death—a situation present in many of the underdeveloped countries today. Ricardo rejected this overpessimistic view for the industrializing countries, maintaining that with proper husbandry and agricultural policies, as well as claiming new lands for agricultural expansion, the Malthusian prediction can be prevented. Say, focusing primarily on industrialization, sought to interpret Smith's "invisible hand" in scientific terminology comparable with his time and therefore formulated his famous Law of Markets.

With all the honor given to Adam Smith's work, the aspect of international trade, neglected by his readers, was placed in a rational and empirical context by David Hume, whose law of trade balanced imports with exports,[2] indicating the necessity for equilibrium in international transactions, thereby preceding Smith and Say in their stated equilibrium approaches.

J. S. Mill's contribution to economics was most significant, apart from his codifying the existing body of economic thought at the time. As a utilitarian, he stated the reciprocal law of demand in which the prices of traded goods are determined in international markets. On the basis of Mill's *Principles of Political Economy*, the development and expansion of such concepts as international indifference curves and contract curves could be developed—all the more so when this branch of economics became "updated" by the application of Keynesian concepts. Nevertheless, the concepts of Hume expanded upon by Mill, such as the balance of trade and the specie-flow concept, still play important roles in international commercial calculations, albeit embellished with the international multiplier and accelerator and the savings-investment effect.

With increasing international trade due to industrialization and the impact of trade on the domestic economies, the neoclassical economists nevertheless maintained their vision inward in the tradition of their classical predecessors. It is somewhat of a historical paradox, therefore, that Keynes, who was so important in establishing the postwar International Monetary Fund and recognized the necessity for dynamics in the area of international commerce, exerted little influence over his followers, the majority of whom continued to keep their focus on the national economy. The consequence is that the businesspeople went in the direction that fortune and their fortunes would take them, entering foreign markets and establishing multinational companies (or transnational companies, as Herman Kahn calls them),[3] while the majority of economists view trade as secondary to the domestic economy. The result is that this concern for looking inward to the national economy to the neglect of international vision has given de facto confirmation in our time to the sentiment expressed by Jacob Viner in 1937 that the theory of international trade as developed by Hume and Mill—apart from the contributions made to customs union theory—still is, in general lines, the predominant theory; apart from

Keynes's contribution, no strikingly different mechanism has yet been convincingly suggested.

COMMENTS ON THE ACCEPTED APPROACH TO TRADE: ON DYNAMIC EQUILIBRIUM

In the aftermath of World War II it is no wonder that the concern of the world's political leaders has been to maintain international stability. The necessity of economic stability and its importance for political stability had been brought home during the worldwide crisis of the Great Depression. Hence, postwar there arose international monetary bodies and trade agreements to ensure that the world's economies would interlock and that industrialized nations would exert pressure on each other and on emerging nations to ensure that the conditions that had led to the rise of dictatorship and demagoguery during the depression years would not come about again. Fixed parity rates for the strong world currencies were established to prevent the wildly fluctuating rates known before the war. This was an especially important move for the reconstruction of Europe and Asia because it sought to prevent the unstable situation that had existed after the Great War—in other words, it sought to prevent history from repeating itself. This move, combined with the politics at the time, was successful because it allowed world tensions to cool to a cold-war situation, where allies in combat became diplomatic enemies and wartime enemies diplomatic allies; nevertheless, it provided sufficient reconstruction and stability to establish the necessary climate for economic development and growth.

When the majority of the wartime countries had achieved sufficient economic independence and prosperity, they abolished the parity exchange rates and allowed their currencies to "float," thereby reaching their exchange rates on the basis of supply and demand for the currencies and for the countries' goods and services. A consequence of this is that speculators in arbitrage have been reaping significant profits as currencies fluctuate according to the short-term changes in political and economic fortunes, both internationally and domestically, bringing gold periodically into style as the magical underwriter of the world's economies.

However, the problem is not one of floating currencies; nor is it a problem of changes in fortunes both domestically and internationally. The difficulty lies primarily with the approach to trade. Speculation in international currencies is just one aspect of trade, and here the stakes are played for the common denominator, money; this immutable fact holds, regardless of the storms that blow, for the sake of maintaining a populace in a relative state of quiet and the basis of power in a stable condition.

There are two approaches to trade. One, the current approach, is based on the Hume-Mill-Keynes school of thought and emphasizes trade as a consequence of economic growth in equilibrium in which individual differences among the nations' economies are exploited through trade, thereby maintaining a general equilibrium among the nations and allowing the exploitation of each nation's trade potential. The second approach views the world's economies in terms of disequilibrium in which the dynamics are generated by the various industries within the economies as a result of innovation and imitation, and their products are the goods and services of international commerce. (This approach is discussed in the next section of this chapter.)

The current approach to trade, that of dynamic equilibrium, is based on the assumption that the domestic economy achieves its best growth rate when in equilibrium, so that changes in infrastructure that result from industrial advances and bring about changes in liquidity holdings and plant orientation do not exert any great disruption in the macro growth pattern that is due to the government's action of "ironing out" disturbances. The effect on international trade is that the balance of payments of countries so engaged tends to equilibrium, with each country's aggregate imports equalling (in Hume's Law) aggregate exports as any imbalance is offset by the debtor countries' currencies (thus echoing the disreputed mercantilist doctrine).

Claim on a trading country in the form of holding its currency brings about temporary disequilibrium in the debtor country, since the reports of this indebtedness reflect an unfavorable balance of trade (again, mercantilist language) and a weak balance-of-payments position that demonstrates the country's low performance on the international markets. When the United States announces a quarterly deficit of many millions of dollars, for example, pressure is put on the currency because its holders tend to sell out for currencies stronger in the international arena; the currency holders thereby weaken the dollar that much more and increase claims on the U.S. economy through the accounting procedure of the national balance sheet, which acknowledges the debts involved. The new holders of the U.S. currency—those who bought it at the low rate—now have a claim on the economy. This sets off an international balancing mechanism as the U.S. goods become cheaper with the dollar weakened in relationship to other trading currencies. The result is that more U.S. goods are sold internationally, with the imbalance rectified by the increased amount of goods and services transacted at the lower international prices.[4] Hence, the United States experiences an increased aggregate trade level with more foreign currencies being accumulated by the United States. The United States thus strengthens its trading position and reduces its unfavorable balance-of-trade position with respect to its partners—a process that places another country as low trading partner with weakened currency. In this manner, the disrupted equilibrium is maintained, moving around an equilibrium position, and since this is expected, the nations' growth patterns are not subject to severe disruptions and internal equilibrium is maintained.

Tariffs are computed as costs with total costs fluctuating with the changes in demand and the holding of foreign debts. Moreover, a country can be both a creditor and a debtor country to different partners in trade, but in the long run the system is maintained in balance, barring all international military conflicts that halt trade and disrupt economic activity.

The closest situation to free trade, in which balance-of-payments equilibrium and domestic equilibrium are emphasized, is that of the customs union. In this economic union its members abolish tariffs, supplementing them with production quotas and predetermined pricing that are justified in allowing the ease of trade. Thus, as customs unions exist today—comments are made on this later in the chapter—members produce competing products so that as quotas are met, surplus production is exchanged for goods and services of nonmember countries at higher prices protected by tariffs. Should surplus products be exchanged for products from other countries' protected industries, they are done so at a comparative advantage due to the quota system and payment for surplus storage as a means of trade. On this point the customs unions gain; because they allow for this kind of production instead of diversifying and competing internationally as a single economy, they lose the resources and storage capacity, building up further the infrastructures of the members and the initiative for managerial competition necessary to remain fully competitive. Protected economies are poor substitutes for the free-for-all competition of international commerce. Whatever national comparative advantages existed before membership, these have been either eliminated or at best reduced as equality and equilibrium are stressed within the union, with the production quotas set by a central planning authority.

This comment is not a criticism of customs unions per se; it merely shows some of the difficulties of maintaining the contemporary approach of dynamic equilibrium in international trade. This entire approach neglects the comparative differences among economies as determined by the products innovated and imitated in the movement of the business cycle. For customs unions, dynamic equilibrium emphasizes the similarities among its members and not so much their differences. It thus places customs union members in a situation of conflict because they operate de facto in a situation comparable to their economic systems of managerial economics. This means that each is in its unique business-cycle stage. By opting for membership in the customs union, countries trade off part of their economic growth and independence for the security of the dictates issued by a planning board whose authority in economic matters becomes the law of the land.

With respect to trade in general the equilibrium approach is no longer relevant. While academics teach this theory and government economic advisers expound upon it, businesspeople behave in another manner. They maintain their activities in a state of dynamic disequilibrium, phasing out marginal products and introducing innovative products and entering imitative markets where the profit margin sustains such action.

Nevertheless, some aspects of the old theory still have influence on the contemporary trading procedure. Tariffs, for example, protect industries from competition; yet multinational companies for the most part avoid tariffs by entering into production in the host country and providing employment and paying taxes, as do the domestic companies in exchange for the abolition of tariffs on products that they produce in other countries and that the host country imports. The profits are eventually returned to the base country; much still needs to be known about this developing form of enterprise. The planning is conducted by the board in the base country, with the branch firms executing the projects in their countries according to the conditions of the host countries. The base management usually allows some leeway in initiating innovative and imitative products, according to the market conditions in which they exist and operate. Tariffs, in short, are obsolete in host countries that contain several multinational corporations but remain, however, as vestiges of the old theory, with throwbacks to mercantilism.

INTERNATIONAL TRADE AND DYNAMIC DISEQUILIBRIUM

If it did not engage in international commerce, an economy in which there is no lack of natural resources and industries to use them would not be operating efficiently. Since advantages among the world's economies are comparative and absolute, natural resources, time, and productivity in this economy would be used inefficiently with respect to economies that produce competitive goods and services at lower costs and lower consumer prices. Self-sufficiency and the bigness of industry are important, of course; more important is the knowledge of utilizing the productive factors at the greatest utility for trading specific goods and services with other countries: This, then, is the purpose of international commerce in the contemporary economic setting.

Hence, the view that the world's economy is one big, integrated system with each sector engaging in a form of specialization is incorrect. This view imposes on the world's economies a Smith-like vision in which the economies are divided into factories with labor units specializing in the products they can turn out at the lowest costs and highest profits. This view is negated by the contemporary world economy, for in this Smith-like view there are no major business cycles, no disruption of products due to innovation, imitation, and the phasing out of production lines, with competition regulated by a deus ex machina in the form of the "invisible hand." Such a view is in complete violation of the realities of contemporary economics and the facts of international trade.

Even during periods of relative quiet and general prosperity the competition on the international markets is intense, for the industrialized countries continue to undergo their unique dynamic changes as firms innovate, imitate, and phase out products. These dynamics cannot be contained within the borders of a trading country, especially when costing factors make the production of one type of product in a country uneconomic and channeling productive resources into other lines will realize greater profits, while at the same time the product is suitable to the industrial production base of another country that enters the first country's markets and underprices and offers a product that meets market demands.

It is significant to note that much international commerce, especially among developing and postindustrial countries—a point treated in the next chapter—occurs because the trading countries are either unwilling or unable to produce each other's goods and services. This task requires the converting of productive capacity to innovative and imitative products at prices lower than those asked by the trading partner, so that each country is encouraged to provide goods and services the other cannot, or is unable to, provide competitively. This usually occurs when the cycle of one competing country is moving higher up the recovery phase than the cycle of another competing country, whose cycle may be moving along recovery or down to recession. The latter country experiences the difficulties of competition for established markets, with innovation occurring marginally with regard to the rest of economic activity.

When competition is sagging and industry is unable to meet its rigors, then government backing is required for the country's position to be reversed. Government backing must not take the form of protectionism, for protection merely results in the competing country's industries raising their prices at the rate of change incurred by the tariff increases, making the product prices still lower but covering the costs of the tariffs. Such support should take the form suggested here because that industry is experiencing recession and is therefore weakened in international competition.

Of course, the necessity is to meet the competition generated by international commerce. For the industrialized economies this competition means providing products of high quality at competitive prices that can be exported to competing countries for different products that can be produced at lower costs and also of high quality. This does not mean that the same goods can be traded, since imitation is not limited to domestic production but is also a factor of international commerce. International imitation is a function of quality and "foreign appeal"—the managerial exploitation of the products' sociocultural environment, as it were, in the use of the products. Depending on the emphasis, if the element of foreign appeal can be exploited sufficiently, prices may rise without influencing sales; such a feat depends on skilled management and advertising. In competition with this approach, the domestic appeal tactic can be equally skillfully employed.

Trade described in terms of dynamic equilibrium is invalid in contemporary economies. Firms engaged in innovation and imitation do not limit their products solely to the domestic economy, so that the dynamics of disequilibrium are generated in the international arena. In this sense, the managerial law of markets is also in effect because production is also geared to foreign consumption and the quantities of products are therefore computed for both types of markets. As each country undergoes its business cycle according to the developments and conditions within its economy, the general trade cycle patterns among the trading countries are closely in phase, for each country seeks the others' liquidity. This does not mean that individual cycles are necessarily synchronized in an international pattern, for living standards, population percentages of pioneering and sheeplike consumers, and liquidity allocation are important factors to be considered. But as economies have become historically interrelated due to postwar reconstruction and as international markets have expanded, the cyclical position of one economy exerts a bearing on the others' economic positions. An economy undergoing recession, for example, will not be able to afford the purchases of another country's products at the prerecession rate, so that the exporting country must cut back output; the cutback may have an impact on its employment level, leading to reduced aggregate liquidity and hence lowering purchasing levels. Of course, the economy may be able to absorb this reduced demand and rechannel production to other markets. Nevertheless, this specific market will no longer be viable for the duration of the importing economy's recession, and compensation must be found for this lost market.

Hence, in light of contemporary economics there are two tendencies in international trade, often with conflicting consequences. First is the tendency to supply a trading partner with products that have been indigenous to the economy in the short run due to successful innovation but that are lacking in the partner's economy. Should the importing economy be managerially oriented, it will possess imitative ability and thereby prove to be a potential competitor with the exporter.

At first, imported innovation provides the exporting country with a comparative advantage—a term correctly applied—in contemporary economics. This term refers to technological and employment mixes which can overcome the resource problem for the postindustrial society—with the product operating with the same dynamics as it does domestically, drawing the liquidity of target consumers. If successful, the product is met with domestic imitation and thus reduces the liquidity flow to the innovative country. This product's impact of course depends on the receiving country's business-cycle position, with consumer liquidity dependent on the position and the domestic economy's ability to respond with imitation also a function of the cycle's phase.

As well as reducing foreign debt by imitating locally, the receiving country may be able to innovate and export this to the same country. The innovation of one country traded for that of another is certainly economically sound, and the imitation generated provides growth for both countries. The imitation is competition, the second tendency in international commerce.

The dynamics of international imitation are the same as those for domestic imitation, that is, market saturation and the phasing out of products no longer profitable or only marginally so. As imitation has filled the markets of one country it most likely has had the same effect on the other; so, the problem is, which country is to reduce its imitative imports to the other? This problem can be resolved by the sales factor, of which the issue of imported versus domestic and production costs is important. Also, of importance is the calculation which must be made between using domestic resources for entering imitative competition against the utilization of these resources for innovation and taking the risks of innovation with the objective of exporting the innovation successfully and earning foreign currency at the innovative rate, thereby gaining on the time span required for imitation to reduce the profit rate. In the first option the international imitation effect assumes cyclic dynamics and so generates an international business cycle that operates in the same manner as a domestic business cycle, although each separate economy in the international business cycle has its own dynamics influencing its position within the cycle and the cycle's movement internationally. Hence, international imitation will reach such an extent that comparative advantages are eliminated and imitation will cease to expand as liquidity is reduced and saturation sets in.

Again, a vital domestic economy can overcome the international cycle by producing for local consumption and relying on the domestic dynamics of innovation and imitation. Employment patterns may be altered, but these can be reestablished in new frameworks of production according to the requirements of the markets. The international business cycle's phases, though relevant and important, are far from binding on a domestic economy. Hence, exporting innovation and gaining foreign currency, although short-run in orientation because innovation is met with imitation, is an important option because it reflects the innovative dynamics in the domestic economy.

These innovative dynamics are also short-term, however, and an economy requires a mixture of innovation and imitation to grow and remain viable. The purpose of trading is to receive products that hold prestige value or are not produced locally or can be purchased as lower-priced substitutes. Competing managers are always confronted with the problem of determining the allocation of resources in the manner yielding the greatest utility. In international commerce, a balance must be struck between domestic production and that geared for international competition. United States automakers, for example, export their automobiles to many countries and have plants around the world; so do Japanese automakers. Yet the consumption of automobiles in the United States leans heavily toward the Japanese models, so much so that at least for the domestic market it may be feasible to phase out domestic production and move into innovative lines of production. The dilemma here is that imitation would bring competitors into these markets as well, eliminating the comparative advantage gained by innovation. The dynamics of international trade and competition are rigorous indeed.

Competition weakens the comparative advantage enough to eliminate it, but this does not mean that competition stifles and prevents or prohibits gaining competitive advantages. Just as in the domestic ring, the prime cause of declining sales is consumer preference. Adaptation to consumer preference is competition; failure to adapt is due to heavy bureaucracy within the various firms. To meet foreign competition firms must offer prices due not to protective measures but to more efficient uses of productive capacity and technology. Quality must be stressed over the use of fantasy and science fiction type advertising. The initial cost adjustment for improving competition must come from the planning room—the managerial drawing board where the decisions are made after alternatives are considered. Thus run the dynamics of imitation, and whether such changes can be implemented depends on the economy's position in the business cycle. If in steep recession with little or no available liquidity, this situation will perhaps be left and other projects evaluated. The country enjoying the imitative advantage thus maintains its competitive edge, selling its product at reduced quantity but still competing more than successfully with the domestic firms. As the cycle moves upward, this situation is altered and the available liquidity allows for the proper actions to be taken and the production program altered accordingly. How the domestic firms bear out in competition thus depends on managerial skills for production and marketing.

Trade in economic disequilibrium is necessary, for it reflects the reality of new markets for innovation and imitation; and where domestic firms phase out products, it allows markets to remain, being supplied by foreign producers. The objective of trade is thus shifted from the Hume-Mill equilibrium argument of obtaining goods by supplying other goods, to the extension of disequilibrium in seeking markets whose production and therefore sales costs are higher or whose firms do not manufacture the products in question. A consequence of this is that trade alleviates the allocation of resources for producing goods and services that can be obtained at lower prices through foreign competition or it allows resources to be channeled into different types of competing production because the markets for these products are somewhat supplied by foreign sources. More resources are left for other uses because of international competition.

In short, the international imitation effect generates in one country another country's innovative and imitative products. This effect is prevalent when the receiving country's cycle is moving upward in recovery or has reached prosperity and as such reflects the sending country's cyclic stage by the fact that the country is producing; most likely, then, the sending country is also in recovery or prosperity, but there is no necessity for this.

Commerce is conducted through the exchange of goods and services and currencies. This was recognized by the mercantilists; hence their definition of a favorable trade balance is exporting more than importing, with the balance compensated for by the other country's currency. This idea has existed ever since, even though the emphasis has shifted to domestic economics. Indeed, it lay dormant to a certain extent during the Great Depression, when the difficulties of one country were exported to its partner in the form of tariffs, quotas, and devaluations. Yet this idea is regaining credence in the current uncertain situation of near-stagnation and inflation internationally, with the gold standard once again considered the basic unifying currency. In this sense the echoes of mercantilism are again heard as the yellow metal flows across international boundaries; the question remains whether gold can really replace national currencies.

Traditionally, money has had three roles. First, it is a means of exchange; second, it is a measure of goods and services; and third, it represents the store of value. Of these neoclassical concepts, only the first is relevant for contemporary economics. To say that money is the measure of goods and services is to reverse the situation, since goods and services, their quantities and qualities, and the utilities they provide determine their measure in money. As a store of value, money's value is not determined by an internal mystique around which the economy evolves; the store of economic value is determined by the economy's productive capacity and the ability to market its goods and services, which in turn depends on their utilities. It is the utility of money and the role of utility in foreign exchanges that are relevant in domestic and foreign transactions.

In international transactions, currency has a double role. As payment for international trade, it can be used in further transactions or held until the international money market raises its value in trading monies as goods subject to the forces of supply and demand. The other role depends on the foreign currency's utility when exchanged for domestic currency. Businesspeople who make such transactions do so at rates that have utility in the country as determined by the demand for the foreign currency over local currency. This ratio depends on the need for that currency to complete foreign transactions and/or on the demand for the currency as a hedge against inflation or political instability. As a unit of accounting, the currency's transaction value is established according to the stipulations of the terms of trade, as an alternative to domestic currency, this depends on its utility in the domestic market as contrasted with the domestic currency, which is determined in part by the cyclical position and by the demand for the currency.

Thus *hard* currency is the most preferred, this being a currency backed by strong industry and stable government and the currency most used for international transactions. For this reason, national currency differs from gold as a universal standard of exchange, for the currency represents the country's industry and stability, both present and in the future. Gold represents the industry and stability of no nation, for it is mined from the ground and stored in vaults. Gold cannot allow for industrial expansion unless its value is fixed to an industrial unit of growth or as a percentage of the interest rate or by any other means of quasi-denomination through substitution. Other than this, gold can have no real role in backing economies in their exchanges.

However, in times of economic uncertainty, such as now, peoples' faith in their national currencies wanes. Because of prolonged recession industry is weakened, the international political arena appears more chaotic than usual, and the echoes of the Great Depression are being heard. People seek a stable currency, one whose store of value in their consideration remains fixed to the relative potential output of international industry; the rise of gold prices against foreign currencies brings back the call to reinstate gold as the world's monetary unit. The problems of the gold standard are known, especially as gold's price fluctuates on the world market as does any other commodity or currency. The question remains, can there be an acceptable international currency?

Although there are acceptable international currencies for foreign transactions, a single currency serving this purpose seems unlikely (the exception is for the customs union, discussed in the next section). A single currency shows no utility nor portrays the strengths and weaknesses of the backing it represents. It will be like gold, a monetary unit to run to in times of uncertainty, having no real industrial support and dependent on the presses—as gold depends on its mining—that controls its supply. The currencies of the industrialized countries are the best for international transactions, for they are backed by their nations' industries and the consumer utilities these industries represent. That these utilities fluctuate with respect to their countries' cyclic fluctuations does not detract from their general utilities with respect to the nondeveloped countries or a nonindustrial gold standard.

A country's currency obtains its utility as a result of sound managerial activity and a government whose policies demonstrate its responsiveness to its country's economic predicament. Hence, the value of a country's currency depends on the country's economic utility both domestically and internationally; this depends on the quality and quantity of industrial output and in the bargaining involved in international transactions for trade.

FURTHER COMMENTS ON CUSTOMS UNIONS

It is easy to construct an economic model in which all the world's economies are engaged in free and open trade. The international imitation effect would move across national borders with much greater ease, unrestricted by tariffs and limited in impact only by consumer tastes and aggregate liquidity preferences. This model represents the best of all possible economic worlds, and yet it is unobtainable in reality. Industrial protection, that is revenues obtained from tariffs, and the social disruptions that would result from the shifting of labor in response to the cyclical movements among the economies, as well as the impact on productive programming resulting from imitation, tell strongly against the allowing of free trade. Indeed, should such trade exist, it would most likely lead to political anarchy and the breaking down of the social systems of many of the countries.

In spite of its lack of reality, the concept of free trade has given rise to the customs union as—to use an expression coined by the late Harry Johnson—the "second best" economic system to free trade. With free trade an impossibility, how effective is the customs union? As a strict economic relationship, the customs union has failed to bring about a new economic order. Since it allows countries to function within the terms of this relationship, it necessarily imposes quotas on their competing industries, which results in the inefficient use of resources and economic distortions. The customs union allows for trade with nonunion members, permitting reciprocal trade for those goods and services that pose little or no competitive threat to the member countries' industries. Full membership in the customs union requires accepting full responsibility; yet, with some countries naturally economically stronger, the equality sought by the union of economies has never been achieved. In its organization the customs union has one commendable point: It allows developing countries associate membership and hence provides a large market for their products. Even here, however, the customs union imposes quotas and tariffs on trade which is often reciprocated by their trading partners which must then engage in imitation to make up for the losses of the products, so that the imitation effect makes them competitors.

As it stands, this last point is insufficient for justifying the customs union's existence. What the union requires is the next logical and practical step, political confederation. This does not imply the denial of national cultures, although a unified culture would most certainly develop over time. It does mean that the economic union requires a political union, with decisions of a political and economic nature taken at a central and agreed upon power base. A difficulty lies in determining which problems are strictly national, that is, local, and which are to be considered by the union's governing body. However, over time, problems relating to a single member will become relevant to the union as a single body—as the Falkland crisis demonstrated for the European Economic Community.

After this step is taken, establishing a single currency is necessary for internal commercial transactions and for international transactions outside the union, if this is agreed upon by customs union members. The interest-rate fluctuations of this currency would be like those in the United States, that is, based on regional utilities of the money. Of course, the element of national pride will have to be overcome, but in the European Economic Community, for example, Great Britain abandoned its traditional currency calculation and went decimal, which was an important step toward currency unification in that customs union. An advantage of a single currency within the union is that as it moves freely among the member countries, it tends to end duplicate and nonproductive production, thereby allowing each country and region within the country to produce according to its comparative and absolute advantages. Another advantage is that it allows for the movement of money without service charges for currency conversions and without the loss or gain in such transactions due to widely fluctuating interest rates. The result is the free location of productive plant and the establishment of businesses in areas most efficient for the production of those businesses as determined by the nearness of resources and markets within the member countries.

Still another advantage of maintaining a single currency for international commerce is that it shows the union's strength as a single identity when foreign transactions are undertaken. Hence, whereas one country may be economically weaker than another, the single currency shows the backing of the entire industrial base of the union, a base that will grow stronger through continuing integration. A single currency will therefore allow more rigorous internal competition and stronger competitive advantages to members when they deal with other nonunion countries.

Put forward as the second-best situation to free trade, the argument for customs unions is that without them, countries tend to become protectionist, taxing imports highly to the extent of willingly or unwillingly supporting local inefficient industries. The theory of free trade is most certainly noble in its orientation, allowing goods and services to move unrestricted across international borders and placing the consumer in the center of economic activity. But because the various phases of the trade cycle in these countries have disruptive effects on international commerce, these cyclic dynamics must be built into the free-trade model to show the chaotic condition that occurs as laborers move freely across borders when the cycle of their country turns downward and makes it difficult for other countries to absorb them into their labor force. The country whose cycle is moving upward is absorbing its own labor force into the economic process, while the country whose cycle is moving downward has great labor mobility seeking employment. The demands of this labor force are reduced because of their position while the labor force of the other country is just beginning to be absorbed. A balance has not yet been struck between the two cycles and hence that labor force with the lowering cycle will not find too many opportunities for work in the other country. In a free-trade model, when one country's cycle is in a lower phase while other countries' cycles are in a higher phase, a disequilibrium results, the consequences of which are the abandonment of this model and the establishment of tariffs and protectionism, as well as the formation of customs unions. Because the free-trade model was never realistic it was never adopted, which is why the customs union, with all its difficulties, is not only realistic and practical but also the second-best condition to free trade.

Customs unions are formed on the basis of geographical location, common political and/or economic interests, and the necessity for controlling the allocation of scarce resources—a definition that indicates that international cartels operate to some extent as customs unions.

The widespread formation of such unions may very well become the future of economics in international trade, especially since the multinational companies are uniting countries economically and since there is strong reaction to cartels. Should this be the future situation, the next step would most likely be for countries to belong to more than one customs union. The subsequent formation of trading blocs would emphasize the best in the economic freedom of trade for innovation and imitation would move freely across international borders, stimulating further innovation and imitation and thus economic growth. This formation of labor blocs prevents the negative social consequences of free-labor mobility because labor could be demanded according to the conditions of each country. It also eliminates the dangers of each country's recession bringing about cutthroat competition in the form of devaluations and tariffs that allow one country's difficulties to be passed to other countries, the result of which would be reciprocal actions that could bring the entire system to a standstill. This argument must not be construed as a plea for a new world order; there have been enough of these pleas and attempts. This is merely forecasting, pointing to a possible evolution of international economics, devoid of utopia or fantasy. The trend is being set by the establishment of customs unions, and with proper managerial skills the second best to free trade can become a viable form of growth, thereby shaping the pattern of world economic development.

10

COMMENTS ON THE DEVELOPING ECONOMIES

> There are truly many roads up each mountain and many mountains up to heaven. Modernization seems increasingly likely to take different paths in different societies.
>
> *Herman Kahn and the Hudson Institute*
> *World Economic Development*

INTRODUCTION

The significance of the enduring question lies in the different ways in which its answers are interpreted in light of different historic epochs. The question of the origins and causes of the wealth of nations raised by Adam Smith is such an enduring question whose issues and problems find widely divergent interpretations and responses today from those of other periods of history.

Smith's question is also applicable to the issues of economic growth and development in countries that compose Western Europe and the non-European countries, such as the United States, that share much of Europe's approach to economics, for these countries have in the course of largely shared histories and mutual contacts formed the systems that compose the economies of managerial capitalism. Although each country has demonstrated a unique approach to its economic situation, an approach largely dictated by historic and cultural developments and the resultant social dynamics, many similarities exist in the patterns of economic growth because of the impact that the Industrial Revolution had made on them. That impact involved industrial development, labor migration to areas that required intensive labor, and mechanism, which led to the reconstruction of the labor force and the development of new skills for coping with the dynamics of industrialization.

The theoretical basis of this Industrial Revolution was provided by Smith's writing. His questioning of the origins and causes of national wealth remains important today, long after the Industrial Revolution shaped Western societies, for the areas of Africa, Indochina, South America, and the emerging and developing countries of the Middle East.

The countries in these non-Western areas are emerging and developing economically but their cultures, in most instances ancient, conflict with development. The question of why these countries were not influenced by the Industrial Revolution in the same period that the Western countries underwent industrialization probes deep into the problem of development, exposing many of the difficulties that confront these countries as they try to achieve the economic standards of the West.

The answer to this question is, to a certain extent, that these ancient cultures did not allow for any great economic initiative on the part of the individual. Before Adam Smith's work, neither did many of the Western countries; it was Adam Smith's emphasis on the entrepreneur in the economic process and the specialization and division of labor in production that broke down cultural barriers and led the way to industrialization. Ideologically, before Adam Smith's work, it was mercantilism in Britain and Physiocracy in France and on the Continent that prevented the development of entrepreneurship. These philosophies tended to dogma in their claim to absoluteness. Part of Adam Smith's genius was that he recognized these positions as philosophies, subject to rational and empirical attack; he argued against these schools of thought from the philosophical viewpoint, and the force of his reasoning together with the revolutionary changes in the means of production resulting from Smith's argument, opened the way to industrialization.

This is not the situation in the emerging and developing countries today, where many of the political systems are political or religious dictatorships or a combination of both, for these systems are not receptive to argument and rational thought and ignore empirical demonstration. It is the combination of religious and political influences in these countries that restricts individual enterprise. Moreover, since these influences are deeply rooted in the cultures of these countries, they largely prevent the political change and ensuing stability necessary to found the proper infrastructures for economic development.

Religion in these countries holds people to powers outside their control and comprehension, making their activities and thoughts subject to forces they cannot understand. Their thoughts and consciences are oriented to an unfamiliar sphere, and entrepreneurial activity stands in direct opposition to this, for it requires the rational exertion of control over resources and their applications in market development. The entrepreneur qua entrepreneur is answerable only to his clients and himself, and these are the forces he understands and with which he works.

Dictatorship prevents deviations from the accepted behavioral modes that have evolved over long periods of time and are deeply rooted in the national conceptualization of the people. These behavioral modes are maintained and enforced by leaders who substantiate their authority on the basis of tradition. Dictatorships, modern expressions of authoritarianism, rely on the imposition of their dictators' ideas by authoritarian methods of enforcement, tolerating little or no deviation, depending on the leaders' characters and the deviations in question. However, while authoritarianism is an evolved form of rule usually accepted by the people as part of the national heritage, dictatorships are imposed by force with social evolution having little or no role in their establishment. There is no rooting in past history nor ideas in the collective psyche justifying dictatorship, making it an alien type of rule, subject to the very forces that placed it in power to overthrow it when the conditions are right. This is due to the personality cult, essential in dictatorships for establishing an authoritarian figure who might have come to the fore through social evolution. This personality cult is as unstable as human passion, and heroes of the state and of the people can become public enemies once they are deposed.

This does not mean that the nations at the time of the Industrial Revolution were free from authoritarianism and dogmatism. The Catholic and Protestant churches had great influence over their followers, but that was a historical situation, differing greatly from the situation of the emerging and developing countries today. The Protestant Reformation and the reaction within the Catholic Church to its own behavior during the Inquisition, as well as the scientific progress made during and after the Renaissance, led to the evolution of a work ethos, separating work from religion by leaving the churches to deal with the needs of the spirit, and work and industrialization with material satisfactions. Although there was most certainly controversy, since the

Inquisition there was never a serious social conflict between material and spiritual needs. Industrialization and religion accommodated each other very well.

Authoritarianism posed no serious problem for industrialization for two reasons. One reason was the impact on society made by industrialization in the form of the radical changes in manufacturing (*manu* meaning hand and *facture* meaning to make) from the tedious process of hand work to the implementation of machinery, which eased the way for accepting industrialization. The emphasis on individual initiative for accumulating the means of output in industry was soon recognized, so that authoritarianism as a dominating social force was shifted from the sociopolitical position of the ruler to the rightful position of the family head. The religious leaders in society yielded their dominating positions to material forces, allowing the social justification and further impetus for inquiry into the sciences and endeavors in the fields of the arts and commerce.

The second reason why authoritarianism was no serious problem for industrialization is that industrialization, with all its ramifications, was not sudden, in the form of a social revolution or rebellion, but gradual, occurring over many centuries. The fertile ground for industrialization was prepared by the changing attitudes toward science and art; so that when the industrial process began and Smith's writing appeared, they signified a new era of political and social development that would not clash with religion and that were greeted with great interest, with industrialization leading to new production processes and opening new markets.[1]

Part of the difficulty of economic development today is the lack of historical time for establishing political stability to nurture the inner dynamism necessary to unleash the forces of individualism required for industrialization. These countries' histories of tribalism and/or religious sects sharing common geographical territory and often at war had been altered somewhat during the era of colonization, when the Christian countries sought to expand their trade and dominance over their neighbors as they searched for better strategic positions and raw materials in distant lands.

The religious beliefs were strange to their colonizers, and the differences in beliefs among the many peoples provided an advantage in controlling them. Missionaries were brought in to unite these peoples in a common belief; this led to exploitation through religion and the force of arms. Not only did this prove an effective way of domination but it also allowed for intrigue among the colonizing powers as they sought to conquer peoples colonized by other powers.

In a very real sense, this situation changed after World War II. Many battles were fought in several of these colonized countries, and their people who served in the armed forces for the most part distinguished themselves in battle, gaining for themselves a new respect. It was put forth that when they were able to adopt the forms of government of their colonizers, they would be granted independence. Independence politically does not, of course, mean independence economically. These countries had achieved a high degree of political sophistication, but their economies lacked integration; their infrastructures were still largely primitive, and the main commercial forces were still controlled by their previous colonial rulers. So long as real economic independence was not achieved, political independence had become merely a sophisticated form of colonization and to some degree oppression.

This situation has become complicated further by the great powers waging their cold war in these very countries. It has become another form of colonization, with puppet governments, controlled by their sponsers, ruling the people. This control is justified on grounds of strategy as the powers seek to outmaneuver each other in sensitive areas of the world. Such a situation leads to political corruption, instability, bloody and bloodless coups, and internal oppression, without any guarantee of economic improvement.

Such has been the fate of the developing countries. In the few developing countries where genuine democracy has taken root, the political soil in which it is planted is still very unstable. Ruling parties have suffered coups and their leaders have been deported, jailed, or executed. Corruption is often rampant, with the sufferers being the nonpolitical populace. Instability is found in the developed countries, but it is a form of instability allowed and nurtured by the system; that of the emerging and developing countries is an instability that leads to revolution, coups, and bloodshed.

The cultures of these latter countries, ancient and important, have not been able to prepare them for the present, so that their political and economic systems do not enable them to produce the goods and services taken for granted in the developed Westernized countries. Amidst all the turmoil is the recognition by both the developed powers and the excolonized countries that a common will and understanding is necessary to rid these emerging and developing countries of the ignorance and poverty that are the main sources of instability. Responsible leaders (as opposed to the barbarian dictators who care only to maintain their personality cult) have therefore sought guidance of the politicians and industrial leaders of the developed countries on how to bring their economies into the latter half of the twentieth century. To the extent that the advice received has been transformed to suit the conditions of their respective countries, it can justly be said that many of these countries are emerging from economic systems totally irrelevant to our time and are developing toward managerially based economic systems, although the road to development is long indeed. The paths up the mountain of growth are determined by the internal conditions and the wisdom of the political and economic leaders.

THE PROBLEM OF DEVELOPMENT

That *problem* is in the singular in the title of this section may seem incorrect; that it should be in the plural form may seem more appropriate, as there are indeed many problems to economic development. However, these many problems can be grouped together under the heading of a single problem, that of applying Western conceptualization of industrialization to the developing countries.

It can be argued that the developing countries should not attempt to adopt the processes of industrialization, that they should undergo their own industrial revolutions and borrow technology whenever it suits their requirements, but that they should not rush industrialization. In this manner their people can adjust to the experience of having their living standards altered and geared for Westernization, since they are active in this transition.

There are difficulties with this argument. First, the dynamics of international politics and conflicts do not allow such development in isolation. The big and intermediate powers vie with each other for territory and strategic positions and often conquer militarily or economically these merging and developing countries, who are thus caught in the whirlwind of international forces and pressures. Second, these countries have problems that cannot be dealt with in such a development process, for their problems are so serious and pressing that they must seek solutions with great urgency. Internally, difficulties of education and welfare and in many instances of poverty abound. These provide fertile grounds for rabble-rousing leading to revolt, especially in those countries where the leadership is not totally responsive to the needs of the people. Often the leadership is overthrown by force of arms, to be replaced by another, likewise unresponsive and dictatorial in persuasion, maintaining the type of system just overthrown yet basing it on greater repression. Moreover, even in the most progressive of the developing countries, internal difficulties render the countries weak enough to tempt stronger countries, thus they fall prey to external domination either by overt military conquest or by economic usurpation, so that their labor force is exploited and their natural resources plundered.

There is simply no time for each country to evolve its own industrial revolution, to develop in its own natural pace; the economic infrastructures necessary for internal economic development cannot evolve rapidly without foreign assistance. Funding and guidance is needed for building roads and providing transportation. Expertise on plant location is necessary for building industries at advantageous locations; educators are necessary for training the people to work the industries. The spin-off of industrialization in the form of improving medical standards and advancing education must be channeled; working for cultural and artistic development, a very crucial area, must be handled by people who understand the impact of industrialization on the country. The acquisition of the managerial skills and knowledge necessary for bringing out the people's enterprising initiative in order to harness the industrialization process and transform it into the most efficient form of managerial interaction, thereby maintaining the momentum and bringing it into new economic areas, is the main problem of economic development. This problem is broken down into many categories, subclasses, and subproblems.

The serious difficulty here is of adapting the assistance from the developed technetronic countries to the cultures and needs of the emerging and developing countries. This difficulty is further complicated because no single mold for importable knowledge can be given as a standard model for development. Certain common needs and requirements do exist among preindustrial countries; apart from these standard situations, however, the differences among the economies are great enough to warrant an *ad hoc* approach in each instance, improvising when necessary.

Peoples with differing conceptualizations can be partners in development only after great adjustment. Hybrid plants, certain vegetables, and new wheat strains known to be rich in nutrients are often rejected as means for coping with nationwide malnutrition brought about by poor agricultural techniques and lack of knowledge for efficient water control. This rejection is due to the adherance to traditional eating patterns, often based on religion, by peoples receiving these foodstuffs. Indeed, when new foods in abundance coexist with malnutrition, then tradition and the newness of the food are often in conflict.[2]

Glamorous schemes that are not properly researched but exist for the de facto function of adding to the government's prestige often result in inefficient uses of resources and long-term destruction. Dams for channeling waters often lead to improper irrigation and the failure to harness these waters for electricity efficiently. Egypt's Aswan Dam, for example, has resulted in the destruction of the sea life necessary for the ecological balance of the Nile; it has also proved harmful for the irrigation of far lands that had been fruitful since antiquity. Some countries have hastily built smelters and now annually report high quantities of steel output, but their product is so inferior and inadequate that they must import foreign steel at great expense. Projects such as these, impressive but incorrectly applying technology and employing people who lack technological competence, result not only in inefficiency and often irreparable damage but also in the loss of needed foreign currency, for the money wasted on the projects and the lack of economically advantageous results must be made up through the goods and services purchased abroad.

MANAGEMENT AND ECONOMIC DEVELOPMENT

Who but a person born, raised, and educated in a country understands the problems of the country? What improves the perspective of such a person more than receiving further education outside the country? This personal training can be divided into two stages, the first stage being his education within the country; the second, the further education on foreign soil. The first stage acquaints the person with the temperament of his people and his own reactions and thoughts as shaped by his cultural environment, while the second stage, being more abstract, acquaints him with the world and the broader issues of international politics. Thus, he becomes a student familiar with the general theories of economics and sociology, with the forces of history and how they shape the world, and with his own country.

The student must acquire managerial knowledge and if necessary be supported by his government as he learns Western technology so that he can understand Western problems and reflect on his own national situation in light of the education and training he receives in the Westernized country.

The acquisition of managerial skills is insufficient in itself, for sociological theories must be learned, together with pure and applied economics and technology. The educational program must be comprehensive and not related specifically to developing countries. The managerial student must, therefore, be given managerial responsibility, either in government or in industry.

Traditionally, postindustrial countries have provided aid to the developing countries directly to their economic sectors, with a twofold rationale for so doing. First, it is considered that the fastest way of accumulating funds to finance government-approved projects is to channel these funds directly into these projects and account for these funds in the government's budget. This policy is based on the economic adage that if the short run is taken care of, the long run will take care of itself. These countries are unable to undergo rapid growth in a short period of time, so that the added liquidity to the economy by means of short-term funding will spur production and assist in building industry, both in the short- and the long-run. A sufficient liquidity ratio from this money and from the money generated within the economy from production and consumption will stimulate an aggregate savings-investment function and a consumption pattern that will become sufficiently strong to enable an efficient banking and marketing infrastructure to develop. From these will follow the availability of loanable funds at reasonable business rates; once availability is established, economic development will be under way, with the patterns of cyclical fluctuations setting in.

Second, the direct method of aid is important, even though the wastefulness it tends to engender is a point of ridicule among the recipients and it is a means of abusing the newly found wealth that this aid furnishes. The "big-power game" that directs important aid engenders instability among the rulers of these recipient countries and opens leaders to the temptations of corruption and big-power influence. These countries are susceptible to coups and proxy rule. These are, nevertheless, the facts of economic development that grew out of the post-World War II urgency to place emerging and developing countries on a solid economic basis to provide stability and to end the causes of exploitation brought about by poor management and dictatorial, authoritarian and nonenlightened religious domination.

In retrospect and in terms of current events, it can be seen that this twofold rationale has not led to all the results intended. In many instances Westernized methods are implemented without their necessary adoption to suit the country's unique conditions. Money is often distributed to recipient countries without its utility considered. Furthermore, many of the recipient countries are still being used as pawns and as sources of energy and power; yet they are playing their roles and altering their allegiances to their own economic and political advantages—many client states are in fact the masters. The consequence is that many of the Indochinese countries and those in Africa and South America are unable to solve their problems and their economic systems are unable to achieve real growth patterns based on industrialization, internal consumption, and viable exporting. As a result, the lack of industrial efficiency of these countries, their pernicious poverty, and their inflation maintain their need for aid—which is never apolitical—and prevents the establishment of an infrastructure sufficient for economic growth.

The student, mentioned earlier in this section, can therefore become an important factor in economic development. The emphasis in his education must be placed on his adapting Westernized concepts to the conditions of his country. The student will confront the difficulty of long training and studying, which will be further compounded by his uphill struggle to abolish old and traditional work methods and establish the methods he has learned. One important fact that the student manager will learn and that he must emphasize at home is that the correct approach to economic development is not one of the percentages of the GNP necessary for the take-off, nor is it dependent on broad ideological theories or support from the big powers to establish development. It is the human element in the economy that has to be put to work efficiently, and this can be done only by the application of sound managerial policies adapted for the country's conditions, its geography, its climate, and the cultural heritages of its people as they aspire to the benefits of development.

DEVELOPMENT AND THE UNIFYING APPROACH: THE ARGUMENT FOR A MIXED ECONOMY

With industrialization the Western countries underwent an evolutionary process: The entrepreneur became the source of economic activity and the governing officials were placed in the position of guarding the rights and the privileges of the citizenry in the wake of the abuses of entrepreneurial activity. As industry developed governments drew up the limits constituting fair game for entrepreneurs as well as protecting the entrepreneur's rights against the citizenry's outcry where such protection was necessary. Further industrial expansion led to the alteration of working conditions and additional legislation was enacted to cope with these changing conditions and times. The consequence of this development and evolution is a mixed economy, with industry providing economic growth and government underwriting economic activity in the private sector as well as underwriting those public utilities that industry is unwilling to supply or is prevented from supplying by legislation.

The argument over government intervention in the economy versus private enterprise in all aspects of economic activity cannot be dealt with here. The problems of developing countries differ greatly from the problems of the postindustrial era; so do the role of the government and the role of the entrepreneur-manager as the source of generating growth through innovation and imitation in these countries. For the developing countries industrialization cannot be an evolved process; it must be imposed, especially as time is pressing and the political and social dynamics in these countries are far from static. Given that each country is unique, what general format can be provided for development that has utility for each developing country?

Such a format must combine management that is essential in industrial planning (the influence of Westernized thinking) and on the government level. A committee of trained people must be set up at the government level to handle foreign assistance, among other things. Another overlapping committee is necessary for planning a proper infrastructure of the highest utility for development. The overlapping itself has utility, for it allows the channeling of foreign assistance into the formation of an infrastructure and the capital equipment that must be worked within it. Furthermore, aid is commonly thought of as monetary financing, Even though aid takes this form to a large extent, aid also includes foodstuffs and working capital equipment, and goods and services that have immediate or near-immediate impact on consumption and production. Aid may also include the nontangible services such as education, whose payoff is not immediate but realized over the very long run. Moreover, capable people are required to formulate guidelines for distributing aid—guidelines that must be rigid enough to prevent anarchy from entering the distribution programs and to prevent corruption in the distribution process; yet it must be sufficiently flexible to account for the unexpected and the human element in the plans. The planning board should be either at the ministerial level or under the aegis of a ministry. This is a delicate job, subject to nonauthorized ministerial pressure, especially in those governments coveting elite classes. Serious governments interested in development —not those run by megalomanics or reward seekers in the big-power game—will treat this committee as an important body in the development process. Moreover, this committee and that responsible for infrastructural planning must cooperate, since much of the funding comes from the aid committee.

The infrastructural planning committee's job is very difficult. It must consider the peoples' temperaments and must project changes in national temperament as development proceeds. The committee must also consider the peoples' impact on development and the directions development will take as the infrastructure is being established. These points bear directly on the nature of the infrastructure, the locations of industry, and the length of time for building both industry and its infrastructure, as well as on the ordering of priorities for the distribution and utilities of the funds.[3]

It is proposed here that the type of government-economy relationship most efficient for the developing countries is a mixed economy in the form of the developed Western countries. This is not to argue that what is good for the countries already in the technetronic era is also good for those undergoing industrialization now; the argument here is that a rigid economic structure of the state-run economy does not allow for the formation of private initiative and the establishment of entrepreneurial activity, with innovation and imitation bringing the economy into the cyclic pattern of growth. Neither can a free-enterprise economy harness the necessary infrastructure within the time pressure of growth for developing the industrial and infrastructurial processes. A mixed economy can offer the best of these forms within the context of each country.

A strong centralized government will establish a plan for growth and either perform to it rigidly or treat it as it sees fit; where little or no deviation is allowed, the plan becomes the growth process and does not act as a guideline. Too loose reins on the growth process leads to economic anarchy and the lawlessness that accompanies it. An objective of the plan should be the harnessing into workable form the most basic of the country's natural resources, these being the talents, the skills, and the physical and intellectual abilities of the people, and to employ these resources in the industrialization process and in the consequences of industrialization.

The plan must establish the necessary productive plant and transportation according to the geographical lay of the land and in relation to the relevant natural resources. Allowance must also be made for the growth of auxiliary businesses servicing the country's main industries, these auxiliary businesses should be privately owned and controlled, subsidized if necessary, and given low-interest loans if required.

The plan should also establish guidelines for taxation as a means of monetary control; taxation should, under no circumstances, be prohibitive. The problems of inflation are likely to set while as money is injected into the economy and industrialization proceeds because this money has little of its utility based on internal production. Because the GNP is likely to be very low during the early stages of industrialization, inflation will increase as prices rise to absorb wages and other income sources. Taxes should be low and encouragement should be given to all businesses and industries as they enter markets and bring about reduced inflation through production and profitable employment in a manner yielding utility.

The master plan should, as nearly as possible in the development process, stress individual initiative. A banking system must be established and savings encouraged to make funds available for entrepreneurial activity. The money accumulated by the banking system will also build reserves for banking in the less-developed areas as development expands and entrepreneurial initiative brings businesses into new regions. Low-interest loans should be granted in the early stages of projects based on sound reasoning and potentially high utility for the development area concerned; this will most certainly encourage natural talents and abilities to be expressed in the development process.

During the early stages of development the criteria for granting low-interest loans and subsidies cannot be rigid. Projects such as textile plants and the rehabilitation of land based on proven methods and sound managerial planning must be supported, for they are labor intensive in the early stages and thus provide employment and income. Auxiliary businesses developing in conjunction with the main industries in the area—together with secondary industries that move the industrial production to the markets—should be backed by either the government or the banking system. The application of knowledge in the form of technology, adapted to the country's requirements, has a role that cannot be emphasized enough. Historically, the introduction and adaptation of this technology to the country's needs results from managerial training received in the postindustrial countries. This technology will become integral to the many sectors in the economy and will be modified as people receive work training in the various industrial sectors. Secondary and auxiliary industries will begin operating within the existing infrastructurial framework and will expand and develop in sophistication as their inventories increase and as consumer sophistication develops as a result of the economic activity and varied consumer choices. After this stage of development is reached, international imitation will take hold and the business cycle, with consumer saturation and shifting markets, will set in. With the establishment of the cycle, the dynamics of managerial economics will be well formed and the development process will be under way.

What can be said about the manager's role in the developing economy? Very often people chosen for further education abroad are selected for specific jobs and must fulfill their obligation upon returning. This is understandable, for the developing countries, having only limited funds and being short on hard-currency, select people for advanced education who have the potential for comprehending the complexities of development. This selection should not be based on pragmatic considerations entirely, however, for development is a long-term process that depends on sound management and the proper utilization of talent and resources. By sponsoring proven intellectuals for further education without obligation, a developing country channels these intellectuals–now an important resource–into private enterprise that adapts Western techniques to the local conditions and temperament. The long-term consequences of this process, that of acquiring local industrial output based on Western technology and employing local ingenuity, cannot be discounted. Such adapted technology, based on Western techniques and developed for the needs of the developed countries, has been adopted by other developing countries because it is closer to their needs and requirements. The technology "shock" reflecting the domestic gap between the preindustrial and postindustrial countries can thus be reduced by technologies of the developing countries, which have more significance for the countries undergoing growing pains.

A two-tier system for managerial selection can be established that obligates one group of managers to work for the government upon completion of their studies while leaving the other group free to find employment upon returning home. Managers who are obligated will lend their talents and training to the formal side of development, drawing up government plans and overseeing their executions. The nonobligated managers will be responsible for aiding the development of private industry; both managerial groups will assist in developing the country's arts and sciences and the socioeconomic infrastructure. Often the free managers are idealists who tend to settle in the more remote areas of the country once the infrastructure for transportation and communications has been established to provide the basis for industry there. Their personalities and inner dynamism give credence to their pioneering and encourage further government support for others to undergo such training for the country's benefit.

Of the system and the personalities working with the system, these factors should be considered with the master plan of growth, allowing further education to those showing promise and merit. Moreover, this plan should allow for direct government intervention in economic affairs, but at the same time providing legal safeguards for individual rights. The calamities of dictatorships should be a warning that a master plan that accounts for all aspects of economic planning is self-defeating and allows little or no real development. This is so because the human element in such a plan must be reduced to a planning factor without being allowed to deviate according to understanding and/or conscience. Because the individual generates economic activity, expression must be given for allowing the plan's general objectives to be worked out, taking into consideration the human element, both as a worker, a manager in a big industry, or the manager of an auxiliary business.

The absence of a master plan for growth may hinder economic development. The developing and emerging countries cannot afford to evolve in a manner similar to the patterns of the postindustrial economies; so, the time-factor for growth should be shortened as much as possible to emphasize the most rapid rate of industrialization and the gaining of technological acumen. The master plan is therefore a necessary substitute for the evolutionary process of development, with the benefits of growth the goal and the negative consequences eliminated as much as possible by the terms and qualifications stated in the plan.

Hence the plan seeks to eliminate the anarchy of uncontrolled development, and if structured properly, it can become a political document ensuring stability and thus reducing greatly the possibility of upheaval and the establishment of a dictatorship. A proper balance can be struck to allow the level of government control necessary for channeling resources and constructing needed infrastructure while allowing individuals free expression and contributions toward their personal welfare as well as toward the good of the country.

The plan, allowing for the establishment of a mixed economy, merges the private and public sectors in a manner similar to their relationships in a postindustrial society. Thus, at the early stages of growth the plan provides the structural blueprint for building up communications, transportation, and the health and education systems so vital for bringing the economy into the latter half of this century. This also provides employment and brings liquidity into the economy through wages and savings, thereby stimulating consumption and production for profit. On the basic level, entrepreneurs take advantage of this liquidity, forming managerial plants that seek to establish markets and expand production for profits, thus forming a supply-demand relationship similar to that of the postindustrial enterprises. Government plants and businesses will take advantage of workers' skills and talents in the building of the country. Both private and public businesses will tend to exploit workers, since no unions will exist at the early stages. However, this exploitation will be offset by worker mobility and the opportunities that exist as soon as the economy begins operating within a market framework.

Although labor unions will no doubt evolve with the increase of the GNP and national affluence, until and after such time, individual rights should be protected by law within the context of the master plan; this is essential for good relations between the private and public managerial classes and the laborers. The threat of exploitation tends to break down the economic system, leaving the economy open for sabotage and revolution. A full, responsive, and viable plan can reduce the potentialities for flare ups that occur in the undirected evolving circumstances of economic growth.

The master plan allows for guidance, establishing the private and public sectors within a working infrastructure, and provides full expression for managerial talent necessary for moving the economy onto the business cycle by innovation and imitation. Once the cyclic pattern is firmly established in the economy, its dynamics will operate in the same manner as those of the postindustrial countries, allowing for the phasing out of marginal products, the planning and manufacturing of new products, and the entering of established and profitable imitative markets. Hence, as the economy develops, so will innovation and imitation expressing dynamic disequilibrium.

The intricacies of the postindustrial economy are so complex that economic evolution is far too slow and painful to be relevant in this half of the century. The need is to speed growth, and the master plan serves this purpose by establishing a mixed economy using natural talent and exploiting the country's resources and political position for obtaining assistance. So urgent is the need for development that the slowly developing countries are sources for international power plays and threaten the possibility of military conflict. A fully cyclical economy will bring about the benefits of the technocratic era, ridding the world of hunger, poverty, and illiteracy. The unifying approach of the managerial and managed mixed economy in the developing and emerging economies will place these economies in the realm of producing and consuming goods and services and placing their products in the arena of international trade.

NATIONAL INDEPENDENCE OR NEOCOLONIALISM: FURTHER COMMENTS ON TRADE

Accompanying the better understanding of the developing countries' problems in the 1960s was the slogan Trade Not Aid.[4] The rationale was that through trade the developing countries would stimulate industrial activity, thereby providing employment and acquiring sophistication enough to become economic partners and competitors instead of recipients of aid. Also, there was the increasing suspicion (often proved to be based on fact) that much of the aid so generously provided went to fill the coffers of the ruling officials and did not find its way to those who were in need of assistance. With trade, much of the corruption was to be removed while industry, supported by foreign demand, would provide employment and internal liquidity leading to consumer sophistication. According to the meaning of the slogan, trade was the generator of internal development and a means of bringing the economy into the age of industrialization.

However idealistic the slogan, the question is, what to trade? Certainly the goods and services of the developing countries are no match for those of the postindustrial societies and any terms of trade that include the products of these countries is only charity in disguise. Under such trade conditions the developing countries would remain client states and thus be hindered from achieving their economic independence.

The solution to this difficulty has proved a mixed blessing. With the advent of multinational companies whose headquarters are in the technetronic societies, good production can be realized at lower labor and hence lower total costs, even when transportation costs and currency differentials are considered, by the industries of the developing countries. Such production provides these countries with an industrial base built by the postindustrial companies and managed with sophisticated techniques for decision making and production, so that not only do those industries in the developed countries benefit from low costs and higher profits but the emerging and developing economies also benefit from the liquidity gained from production and employment and they acquire a trained labor force skilled in manufacturing. Local management is trained to direct these industries, thereby increasing the rate of development. Allowing for a degree of labor mobility, this training is transformed to other types of firms and production lines, which also benefit from the liquidity brought about by these foreign-owned businesses. Moreover, these businesses pay taxes and donate to charities.

Both types of economy thus benefit from this relationship. It is also the case that the developing countries improve their levels of sophistication, so that further production processes are transferred to the industrial base and thus allow for an increased infrastructure. The postindustrial countries, relieved of this production, channel resources into more sophisticated lines and contribute to the advancement of the developing economies. This allows for the training of workers in the developing countries and foists upon them the twentieth century; it brings them, in short, into the dynamic disequilibrium of the modern era. It is certainly a viable shortcut to development, one with the least conflict and resistance because it involves a great proportion of the domestic economies' resources in economic use and provides high employment levels, since the knowledge gained from such production transfers spreads throughout the developing countries.

The question must be raised, however, is this plan a method for providing economic growth for the underdeveloped economies or is it another form of colonialism, unique to the postwar era? Motives are not in question here, for what may start as purely altruism may in fact turn out to be pure exploitation. Motives cannot be so easily detected. What must be considered, therefore, are the consequences of such a policy.

Part of the difficulty is the lack of an unambiguous definition of the multinational company. For example, does the multinational company include only those companies who deliberately spread their subsidiaries around the world on the basis of a minimum-cost-high-profit ratio? Can a company with one subsidiary in another country be termed multinational? According to the terms of agreement between the developing country and the foreign-based industry, what percentage of profits must be given to the base industry without being considered exploitation or neocolonialism? And what ratio will be fair to both industry and the developing country, considering the risks to the industry, the time required to adjust to industrial production and train workers, and the long-term cost benefits the industry acquires by engaging in innovation and imitation while its products are manufactured at lower costs in the developing country? The industry can build its subsidiaries to manufacture phased-out products in the developed countries, thereby maintaining its production lines, while it diverts its major production to innovation and imitation for the more sophisticated markets. The industry can thus enjoy a favorable cost-profit advantage in the developing countries.

In spite of all the economic advantages, the difficulty is knowing who in the developing country, where a substantial portion of industry is owned by multinational companies, is the *de facto* economic leader. The developing country receives its production projects from the parent company; in the long run, this allows knowledge and technology to be directed toward building up the other sectors of the economy and, given political stability, will lead to the emergence of a developed economy. But can economic independence really be achieved when so many parent companies hold so much influence in the developing country?

Perhaps this matter can be clarified by recent history. Japan, for example, has achieved economic independence; so has Singapore, and apart from a strong military dependence, so has South Korea. These were countries that required large amounts of aid and building in the postwar reconstruction, and in each country there was the necessity to achieve economic and political independence. The rebuilding of Japan has proved to be a valuable investment in the sense that it provides stability in a highly volatile region; Singapore has the same stabilizing influence. South Korea must serve as a bulwark to the Northern part of the divided country and also must remain economically sound and viable to withstand the political and economic onslaught of communist-dominated North Korea. In each case the patron-client relationships between the governments was terminated and replaced with a relationship based on equal partnership and mutual respect. This released the client countries to develop their economies as they saw fit, yet still under the influence of the newly forming multinational corporations based on foreign soil. Together with these multinational companies, the local businesses mustered the local labor forces and provided work, exploiting low labor costs to compete favorably on foreign markets. The consequence of this is the development of local giant corporations in competition with the multinationals and operating on the same soil where the multinational corporations are based.

The influence of the multinationals cannot be curbed, but this is no reason that local government and business leaders have to submit to their influence. Having their business generates employment and income; a mobile labor force can then be employed by local businesses that can adapt to the domestic market conditions as well as generate dynamic disequilibrium through innovation and imitation and thus adapt to the requirements of the international arena. Certainly, skilled political leadership is required to encourage local business and not alienate the multinational corporations while maintaining independence. The level of such skills determines the extent of independence in the process of development and growth.

Can the experiences of Japan, Singapore, and South Korea—as well as the European countries rebuilt after the war—also hold for the African, Asian, and Latin American countries? Circumstances are not the same, and the political climate is certainly different. Can real growth and economic independence be achieved, then, by these emerging and developing countries? Skill, sensitivity, awareness, and ability are most assuredly required by the political and business leaders of these countries. With the power blocs and their "agent countries" seeking out new clients in the big-power struggle, independence and growth are certainly difficult to achieve.

Those developing countries that have not fallen under one of the big-power influences, which through skill and maneuvering have managed to remain independent, can assist each other by forming a customs union of trade zones in which labor, goods, and materials can move among the countries without limits, other than what the countries can absorb, free from import duties. Each country can determine the sense in which its participation is feasible and then enter into the customs union agreement. This union should not exist within geographical blocs, and the terms granted to the members should be based on the stages of development, the countries' needs, and the work force available. Such a union would provide employment and international sharing of knowledge, based on the vested interest of maintaining independence while achieving real growth. Markets will then be available for production and the countries' firms can then be brought to the innovative and imitative levels so that the business cycles will be established, moving the economies rapidly to the levels of growth achieved by the postindustrial societies.

As it stands now, the gap between the postindustrial countries and the developing countries is wide, with the differential in changing production brought by the disequilibrium dynamics of market shifts favorable by far for the postindustrial countries. Since goods and services are transferred primarily from the developed to the developing countries and since the money flow in terms of aid is one way, the need is pressing for the formation of a basis for relationships in which comparable market productivity exists and specialization, innovation, and imitation serve as the reasons for the terms of trade. This can best be achieved when the developing countries have established cyclical growth patterns because these are the consequences of market formations, changing consumer tastes, and utilities and liquidity ratios.

Much certainly has to be done, and this is complicated by international tensions. The challenge exists and the struggle for growth and independence is in earnest. The leadership in each developing country must come to the fore to work with both the internal and international forces in building their countries. The alternative is famine, illiteracy, military and ideological war, reliance on the conscience of the developed countries–in other words, more of the same.

NOTES

CHAPTER ONE

1. Thomas R. Malthus, *Principles of Political Economy*, 2nd Ed. (1836), p. 363n.

2. J. M. Keynes, *The General Theory of Employment, Interest and Money* (London: MacMillan, 1947), p. 26.

3. The concept of expectation, though certainly of a psychological nature, was not minimized by Keynes, for expectation influences directly and indirectly economic forces. Money, when entered into circulation, bears on expectations with the nonpersonal forces of economics often dashing the greatest economics to the ground. Keynes devoted an entire chapter to the impact and influences of expectations in economics (cited from Chapter 5, "Expectation as Determining Output and Employment"). Expectation has a central role in *The General Theory*; it also has an important role in the theory developed in this book, although in a context slightly different than that expounded upon by Keynes.

4. Oscar Lange argued that Say's Law precludes any monetary theory, but he draws the conclusion that the traditional procedure of the theory of money involves a contradiction: "Either Say's Law is assumed and money prices are indeterminate—but then Say's Law and hence the neutrality of money must be abandoned." Compare Oscar Lange, "Say's Law: A Restatement and Criticism," in *Studies in Mathematical Economics and Econometrics*, ed. O. Lange, J. McIntyre, and T. O. Yntema (Chicago: University of Chicago Press, 1942), pp. 67-68.

Commenting on Lange's point, Franco Modigliani stated that

> Lange's result seems due to the failure to distinguish between necessary and sufficient conditions. Say's Law is a sufficient condition for the neutrality of money but not a necessary one. Lange asks me to inform the reader that he agrees with my conclusion. This conclusion, however, does invalidate his result that under Say's Law the money prices are indeterminate.

From Franco Modigliani, "Liquidity Preference and the Theory of Interest and Money," *Econometrics* 12 (1944): 45-88, quoted from the above-titled essay in F. A. Lutz and L. W. Mints, eds., *Readings in Monetary Theory* (Homewood, Ill.: Irwin, 1951), p. 217n.

Indeed, this result is invalid, for according to Say's Law the prices are determinate, fixed by the equilibrium position, that is, the point where the supply and demand schedules meet.

5. An example of a noneconomic explanation was given by W. S. Jevons in 1871 when he wrote thus: "It seems possible that commercial crises are connected with a periodic variation of weather affecting all parts of the earth, and probably arising from increased waves of heat received from the sun at average intervals of ten years and a fraction." Cited from W. S. Jevons, *The Theory of Political Economy* (Harmondsworth, England: Penguin Books, 1970), pp. 710-711.

The point that cyclic weather conditions have a rigorous effect on the economy is certainly debatable. What is not debatable is that extra economic activity does indeed affect the economy. The failure of the Soviet crop, for example, led the Soviet leaders to purchase U.S. wheat, thus causing an appreciable rise in the price of bread on the U.S. market due to the relative scarcity of domestic wheat. This rise led to the increases in prices of other foodstuffs; moreover, the supply of wheat to the Soviet Union detracted this commodity from other countries, thus affecting their economies.

The United States' extensive involvement in the world economy had led to the importation of inflation from the United States to other economies and to its reimportation into the United States in the form of higher-priced goods and services, bought because they are preferred to the domestic product. Inflation is also exported in the form of spiraling energy prices, which in turn affect the prices of all segments of the world's economies. How much of this is purely economic and nonpolitical is certainly debatable.

6. Tibor Scitovsky, *Welfare and Competition* (Homewood, Ill.: Irwin, 1951), p. 231. Scitovsky was discussing here neoclassical perfect competition; his argument holds, however, for all forms of equilibrium.

7. Furthermore, Keynes argued that as demand and employment are interrelated, when effective demand is deficient there is underemployment in the sense that there are unemployed people who are willing to work for less than the existing wage rate. "Consequently," Keynes wrote, "as effective demand increases, employment increases, although at a real wage equal to or less than the existing one, until a point comes at which there is no surplus labor available at the existing real wage; i.e., no more men (or hours of labor) available unless money-wages rise (from this point onwards) *faster* than prices." *The General Theory*, p. 289. Effective demand depends on production and the consequent supply, which in turn depends on employment for both production and consumption.

When expenditures increase with full employment, distortions occur in the economy. Keynes wrote that for a while rising prices may delude entrepreneurs into thinking that they are making higher proceeds from sales; as a result, they increase employment beyond the profitability for so doing. Also, entrepreneurs can pass off the rising costs to the rentier, since the rent payment is fixed and affected in real terms by the distortion.

More likely, however, the entrepreneurs will continue bringing new products into the market as inflation alters their profitability position. Should they be unable to continue doing so, either they will phase out those markets that are no longer profitable and bring into the market new products to stimulate demand or they will relinquish their entrepreneurial position and become an imitator, entering into established and secure markets. These points will be discussed extensively in this present work. It is certainly a point Keynes did not treat sufficiently, since the problem area with which he dealt did not allow him to dwell to any great extent on the entrepreneur-manager in economic activity.

CHAPTER TWO

1. Evsey Domar, *Essays in the Theory of Economic Growth* (New York: Oxford University Press, 1957), p. 83.

2. Cited from Zbigniew Brzezinski, *Between Two Ages* (New York: Penguin Books, 1978). He writes that the technetronic society is one

> which is shaped culturally, psychologically, socially and economically by the impact of technology and electronics—particularly in the area of computers and communications. The industrial process is no longer the principal determinant of social change, altering the mores, the social structure, and the values of society. In the industrial society, technical knowledge was applied primarily to one specific end: the acceleration and improvement of production techniques. Social consequences were a later by-product of this paramount concern. In the technetronic society, scientific and technical knowledge, in addition to enhancing production capabilities, quickly spills over to affect almost all aspects of life directly. Accordingly, both the growing capacity for the instant calculation of the most complex interactions and the increasing availability of biochemical means of human control augment the potential scope of consciously chosen direction, and thereby also the pressures to direct, to choose, and to change. (pp. 9-10)

However, one point needs further clarification. The Industrial Revolution was more than a determinant of change, altering the mores, the social structures, and the values of society. The industrial process was and continues to be a political, economic, and social dynamic that provides expression for change through the exploitation of consumer biases and preferences. This provides for the continuous interaction between consumer purchasing and the building and expansion of industry.

3. In discussing the nature of models, Sir Roy Harrod wrote:

> If we want to bring "models" into economics, but to keep them meaningful, we might confine the term to a system of equations, not all of which are tautologies. Some at least might have adjustable parameters. It might be made a condition for the use of the word that some equations explicitly omit to take into account fringe influences. In this sense my system [that is, the Harrod-Domar model] might be called a model, but only if it is taken to include those equations containing adjustable parameters, like the behavioral parameter of the representative entrepreneur of the marginal utility of income schedule.

From *Value, Capital, and Growth*, ed. J. N. Wolfe (Edinburgh: Edinburgh University Press, 1968). Quoted here from S. Mittra, *Dimensions in Macroeconomics* (Random House: New York, 1971), pp. 37-38.

4. Robin Marris, *The Economic Theory of "Managerial" Capitalism* (London: MacMillan, 1967), p. 1. All quotes from Marris are taken from this work.

5. A further distinction between traditional economics and managerial capitalism pertains to the demarcation between economic theory and social theory, which Marris maintains was false from its inception. This demarcation was useful for the development of economic theory because it enabled the focus to be placed on specific issues of economics without complications from involving social dynamics, but in managerial economics this demarcation must be dropped because, as Marris states it,

> a man's utility system is the result of his social situation, of the society around him and of the way it has moulded his psyche. But his social system depends in turn on economic organization. For example, it is by no means obvious that action intended to maximize the utility of a company's stockholders is consistent with maximizing the utility of the action-takers, i.e., of the management. (p. 5)

However, it must be noted that a social system's economic organization results from the very dynamics of the social system itself. Nevertheless, as there is a strong intertwining of these factors, they are extremely difficult, if at all, to isolate or separate.

6. Ibid., p. 184.

7. In this context, G. L. S. Schackle's comment on equilibrium is relevent. He wrote that "equilibrium is a paradox, for in it each rival interest serves itself by offering advantages to all others." From "The Concept of Equilibrium," in *A Scheme of Economic Theory* (Cambridge: Cambridge University Press). Quoted here from Mittra, *Dimensions in Macroeconomics*, p. 67.

CHAPTER THREE

1. A. Charnes and W. W. Cooper, "Management Models and Industrial Applications of Linear Programming," in *Management Sciences* 4 (1957): 38-51. Reprinted in *Managerial Economics*, ed. G. P. E. Clarkson (Baltimore: Penguin Books, 1968), pp. 303-372.

2. This does not necessarily mean that the highest level of diminishing returns must be obtained, for a sophisticated management can detect the slightest decline in profits and determine whether this decline is due to approaching saturation. At this point considerations of new proposals are acted upon and the investigation of future projects for production undertaken. This is the *modus vivendi* for diversification.

3. In the aftermath of the Great Depression the only viable alternative to a capitalist economy, with its basis in Smith's and Say's theories, was the socialist economy, with its government-directed base, as it existed during the war years. This alternative was rejected out of hand and thus left a neo-Keynesian macro economy with its Marshallian theoretical micro base. For both approaches, and in the Harrod-Domar model, the emphasis on equilibrium and growth are historically and theoretically incompatible.

4. Marris, *Economic Theory*, pp. 301-302.

CHAPTER FOUR

1. Joel S. Demski, *Information Analysis* (Reading, Mass.: Addison-Wesley, 1972), p. 4.

2. The potential investor may not become the actual investor, as this depends on his personal inclinations and other information at his disposal. Two investors receiving the same information about a firm's capabilities and future prospects may draw different conclusions based on the total information each possesses. Along with this information, they must consider the personal factor. A high probabilistic rating given in the present about future potential is no guarantee that capital already tied up in investments will be released for the firm in question; this may bring about a trade-off between a certain present and a speculative future, for the investor may prefer to keep his liquidity in its present state and leave his investments untouched.

3. Entropy in physics is defined as the degree of disorder in a physical system. In gases entropy is considered the equilibrium condition in which little definition or activity occurs. This term, borrowed from physics, is used in information theory to mean the disorder, or disinformation, in an information system. A

system that is in equilibrium is also entropic because it does not respond to changes and thus becomes irrelevant to the field for which it was originally destined.

Harold Hotelling used the concept of entropy in "A General Mathematical Theory of Depreciation," *Journal of the American Statistical Association* (1925), Vol. 20.

4. Marris, *Economic Theory*, p. 108.

5. H. A. Simon, "Theories of Decision-Making in Economics and Behavioral Science," *American Economic Review* 49 (1959): 253-285. Quoted here from the same article in G. P. E. Clarkson, ed., *Managerial Economics* (Baltimore: Penguin Books, 1968), p. 26.

6. Marris, *Economic Theory*, pp. 247-248. Variations of this theme are there stated.

7. H. A. Simon, "Decision-Making," p. 28.

8. Keynes, *The General Theory*, pp. 135-136.

9. Ibid., p. 141.

CHAPTER FIVE

1. J. M. Keynes, *The General Theory*, "Introduction," p. 3.

2. Cited from Keynes, *Treatise on Money* (New York: Harcourt, Brace & Co. Inc.) 1930. See Book IV for his discussion on interest and investments.

3. The distinction in this argument between savings and investments is that savings is institutional, for it involves placing money in banking programs and government bonds. Investments pertain to placing money at the disposal of business. In both cases the value of money depends on the supply and demand for liquidity.

Regarding investment (and savings) behavior, Dale W. Jorgenson formulated an approach based on the neoclassical concept of optimal capital accumulation, in which the object is maximizing the present value, be it for an investor or a firm. This value is derived by maximizing utility with regard to what he terms the consumption stream, subject to a fixed set of production possibilities and to fixed current and future prices and interest rates. His argument is demonstrated mathematically and holds for his main premise that investment behavior for a fixed time depends on the maximization of utility as determined by the interest rate—this on the neoclassical consideration that the demand for investment is a decreasing function of the interest rate. He cautions thus:

> However, the demand for investment goods depends on the rate of interest through the comparison of alternative paths of capital accumulation, each continuous and each depending on the path of the rate of interest. Although this conclusion appears to be the reverse reached by Haavelmo, his approach to the demand for investment goods is through comparative statics, that is, of time. The demand function for investment goods cannot be derived by means of such comparisons. As a proposition in comparative statics, any relation between variations in the rate of investment and changes in the rate of interest is nonsensical.

From "The Theory of Investment Behavior," in *Determinants of Investment Behavior*, Robert Ferber, ed. (New York: National Bureau of Economic Research), pp. 129-155. Quoted here from S. Mittra, ed., *Macroeconomics* (New York: Random House, 1965), p. 174.

Certainly utility is of the greatest importance for both investors and managers, but as utility varies over time, so do the concerns of investors and managers and their utility preferences. Utility maximization, subjectively, is strictly a personal approach; but objectively, such maximization depends on comparative dynamics and competing alternatives. Jorgenson's approach, that investment behavior for a fixed time depends on utility maximization during that time, is sound; his argument that the demand for investment is a decreasing function of the interest rate is faulty, for it is not the interest rate which influences investment but the decision to remain liquid or to invest, and it is this decision that has a bearing on the interest rate. His statement could be altered to read that the interest rate is a function of utility; however, this requires dropping the neoclassical premise of optimal capital accumulation, for such accumulation is a function of utility as well.

4. Keynes wrote in *The General Theory* that

> if there is any such rate of interest, which is unique and significant, it must be the rate which we might term the *neutral* rate of interest, namely, the natural rate in the above sense which is consistent with *full* employment, given the other parameters of the system; though this rate might be better described, perhaps, as the *optimum* rate.
>
> The neutral rate of interest can be more strictly defined as the rate of interest which prevails in equilibrium when output and employment are such that the elasticity of employment as a whole is zero. (p. 243)

CHAPTER SIX

1. J. A. Schumpeter, *The Theory of Economic Development*, trans. Redvers Opie (New York: Oxford University Press, 1969), p. 80. All quotes are from this writing.

2. Ibid., p. 78.

3. Ibid., p. 213.

4. Ibid., pp. 243-244, 245.

5. Ibid., p. 7.

CHAPTER SEVEN

1. J. M. Keynes, *The General Theory*, p. 322. In a footnote on the same page, he adds, "For, if we are precluded from making large changes in our present methods, I should agree that to raise the rate of interest during a boom may be, in conceivable circumstances, the lesser evil."

2. A controlled economy whose priorities are set by a high planning board is an example of a managed economy without the element of the profit motive. The economic requirements are established by government in response to the situation. Bottlenecks in production arise without the managerial incentive to remove them and there is the inability to open new markets without the consent of the planning authority. Moreover, there is the tendency to distort production figures when the planning board's requirements cannot be met; so, while production may look on paper to be sufficient, in reality it is deficient. Stockpiling basic production materials is common, for these materials are allocated according to the planning board's calculations and not of those of the manager on the job. These situ-

ations lead to the use of hard currency in conducting international commerce instead of the economy's own industrial output. The employment of hard currency serves as a sign of the lack of international confidence and as hedge against possible future difficulties.

As for the differences among the various forms of dictatorship, these depend on the peoples' national temperaments. In economics, no differences are evident, for the means of production are controlled by the government, with all the diseconomies this implies.

3. A. F. Burns, *Stepping Stones Toward the Future*, 27th Annual Report of the National Bureau of Economic Research, 1947, p. 27. Reprinted in A. F. Burns, *The Frontiers of Economic Knowledge*, 1954, p. 45. Quoted here from R. A. Gordon, *Business Cycles* (New York: Harper & Row, 1962), p. 7.

4. J. M. Keynes, *The General Theory*, p. 313.

CHAPTER EIGHT

1. This is not a disguised version of the underconsumptionist or overproductionist arguments; it expresses the breaking down of the consumer-manager relationship described as the heuristic law of markets. The consumers in this relationship have stated their willingness to allocate their liquidity in other ways, weakening the support for these products through the decline in consumption. This law of markets cannot be a strict relationship; it expresses a pattern of behavior to be sought, but it lacks strict control; nor does it express such control over consumer spending.

CHAPTER NINE

1. Jacob Viner, *Studies in the Theory of International Trade* (London: Allyn and Unwin, 1937), p. 291.

2. This was a brilliant law for its time and foreshadowed Say's Law. The key to the long-run adjustment mechanism is the outflow of gold in payment, thus ringing the death bell for gold and mercantilism, a ring responded to by Smith and still heard today in arguments against the gold standard. While Say focuses on the internal economy, the Scotsman David Hume sought the balancing mechanism for trade; hence, his specie-flow law emphasizing the exchange of goods and services over gold and other specie, that is, his commodity theory.

3. The subject of multinational companies and their influences on the economies in which they operate is in need of much research, both for international economics and for macroeconomics. These companies are formed because of the intrasite workings of managerial capitalism in which managers at high level are on location and the parent company has interests in several countries represented by the managers. A company that has a turnover exceeding $60 million in another country has the beginnings of a multinational company, with the potential to expand into other countries.

Herman Kahn's comments are therefore interesting; using the United Nations' term *transnational corporations*, he lists seven reasons for their growth:

1. Continuation of world peace, relative political stability, and worldwide economic growth (even if it is more like 4 percent than 5). However, there will

not only be a slowing down of the growth of the TNC [transnational corporations] operations in the developed world. This will result in more interest in the developing world and a rapid growth of some operations of current TNCs and new competitors in the developing world.

2. There may be some growth of protectionism that will put greater pressure on the TNCs in the future than in the past to get beyond barriers of trade.

3. In the past, TNCs were often accused but were mostly innocent of locating plants away from the home country to exploit less expensive labor and then re-export back to the home country or to other high cost areas. But this will become increasingly important and is extraordinarily useful for the world as a whole, although it may or may not hurt specific industries in the home country. . .

4. Increasing importance of economies of scale, large amounts of capital, competent management, advances in new technology and skilled marketing. These are just a few of a large number of tasks for which the transnational corporation is ideally suited.

5. Continuing decrease in transportation and communication costs.

6. Momentum from current investment and experience. A number of companies have learned how to operate worldwide and are continually looking for opportunities to do so. A number of others wish to imitate their experience. . .

7. No pervasive or effective interference from political authorities. There is enormous and pervasive criticism, and presumably much of it will continue. However, in many countries of the world, particularly Latin America, the Mediterranean area, and Southeast Asia, there is increasing tolerance at the practical level for the transnational corporation and a greater understanding of the important things they can do than existed a few years ago. . .

Kahn and the Hudson Institute, *World Economic Development–1979 and Beyond* (New York: Morrow Quill Paperbacks, 1979), pp. 250-251.

In Kahn's argument it is assumed that the world's economies operate on a basis of dynamic equilibrium. It would certainly be interesting to see a model in which the dynamics are in disequilibrium.

See also, Richard J. Barnett and Ronald E. Muller, *Global Reach: The Power of Multinational Corporations* (New York: Simon and Schuster, 1974), for a pessimistic approach to the multinational companies. The shifting markets that these writers describe are the closest situation to dynamic disequilibrium; the writers, however, did not find any saving property of these companies. This is an extremely interesting and important work, even though this present writer is in disagreement with many of the ideas and arguments expressed.

4. This is realized in those countries whose currencies have become cheaper internationally by the increase in tourism because they offer better values on exchange–a post-Keynesian justification of sorts for Hume's Law.

CHAPTER TEN

1. Of course, industrialization was not without its serious social problems. The city slums, the polluted living conditions, the paradox of requiring a strong labor force yet subjecting workers to long hours in poor working conditions–all existed. The problem was one not of social inadequacy but of knowing how to handle these

problems while maintaining growth. Hence, while industrialization was in full swing in Victorian Britain, during this period of social conservatism, socialism rose in protest. Also, this explains Schumpeter's entrepreneur carrying out perhaps the most important of economic functions and at the same time being the subject of scorn and ridicule by others.

2. In an essay, "The Konga Experiment: Lessons of the East African Groundnut Scheme," Professor S. Herbert Frankel tells about the troubles and, indeed, the calamities that plagued this British plan. Perhaps the most devastating factor of this scheme was the lack of real awareness of what was being done. To quote Professor Frankel:

> To sum up, I would say that the scheme was, in the first instance, nothing more than an over-large land-clearing operation. It failed to allow for the long period of time which would elapse before knowledge and experience would indicate the most suitable scale and type of organization for economic production in the proposed regions. It took for granted that once the land had been cleared successful agriculture could be immediately established by large-scale mechanization. But nobody yet knows the scale of system of farming which can economically replace the primitive native efforts in these regions.

From *The Economic Impact on Under-Developed Societies*: (Oxford: Basil Blackwell, 1959), p. 152. In an essay in the same volume, he wrote, "Thus one can sum up by saying that the problem of economic development in Africa has in fact ceased to be, if it ever was, a narrow economic question: it is a question of incorporating Africa into the world economy at a rate, and in a manner, which will not endanger the peace and stability of Africa itself." From "Investment and Economic Development in the Continent of Africa," p. 139. His words ring true today and not only for Africa.

3. This point is stressed by Frankel and most other development economists. The building of infrastructure is most certainly difficult; its importance cannot be overstated, for this is the basis for all productive and agricultural industrialization.

4. Slogans are catchy to the ear and sometimes deserve looking into, especially if such as this one they tend to import meaning. But they raise questions for the curious; for example, with this one: What kind of trade, when their economies cannot stand up to our competition? Why abolish aid, why not leave some or all aid programs intact? Of course, this slogan implies that aid should eventually be abolished and trade instated in its place, but this is found only after probing the slogan's meaning. While slogans are appealing, proposals based on understanding are what is wanted.

INDEX

ABOUT THE AUTHOR

David Z. Rich—born in Detroit, Michigan in 1940. Graduated from the Florida State University with degrees in economics and philosophy, did post-graduate studies at the London School of Economics. Works in Israel as an economic consultant to several businesses and multinational corporations and is an administrator to a music conservatory. He has done research in the fields of politics, economics and philosophy.